D1712833

Hestia's House

Blaine Paxton Hall

Hazelhurst House

Hazelhurst House
P.O. Box 5427
Pinehurst,
NC 28374

ISBN 0-9726821-8-X
LCCN 2003102773

www.HestiasHouse.com

All poems herein are by the author, unless otherwise noted.

"Commitment" first appeared in *Oak Apple Thoughts,*
Woodstock Community High School Literary Anthology;
May 1970.
"Intensive Care Unit" first appeared in *They Wrote Us A Poem,*
Volume IV, Duke University Medical Center; Honorable Mention
Award 1999.
The section entitled "Learning the Thunder," in Chapter 10, is
adapted from and first appeared in the *North Carolina Medical
Journal,* January/February 2001.
"What the Shaman Knows" first appeared in *They Wrote Us a Poem,*
Volume VI, Duke University Medical Center; Honorable Mention
Award 2002.
"Here's a Christmas Child for You," first appeared in *The Witness,*
December 2002.

First Edition 2003

Printed in the United States of America

To the United States of America,
my home.

Acknowledgments

My brother, **Phillip Webster Hall,** my cousins **Kathy Harrop** and **Tom Lanning MD,** and my sister **Esther Hall Gordon,** for genealogical information, historical documents and photographs

A.R. Reeder, dust jacket design and photography; restoration and layout of interior photographs

Lynne Peterson, Pre-Press Supervisor, *The Pilot,* my Quark page layout consultant

Ralph Grizzle, Kenilworth Media, for teaching me the tricks of the trade

Linda W. Hobson, Ph.D., past Executive Director of the North Carolina Writers' Network, for editing

Don Peasley & Associates, for research of his photo archives, and permission to use his historic photograph of the Todd School's Grace Hall

First United Methodist Church, Cambridge, Ohio, for historical information about my grandfather, The Reverend Honorable Forest Webster Hall

McHenry County Historical Society, for research

Woodstock Christian Life Services, for photocopies of my archived Woodstock Children's Home personal files

The Weymouth Center for the Arts and Humanities, Southern Pines, NC, for permission to use A.R. Reeder's Boyd House photograph on dust jacket cover

Prologue

My intention is to tell of bodies changed
To different forms; the gods, who made the changes,
Will help me—or I hope so—with a poem
That runs from the world's beginnings to our own
days.

Ovid, *Metamorphoses*

Contents

Part Five
Ground School (1970-1980)

Part Six
Move to North Carolina and Gender Odyssey
(1981-1991)

Part Seven
Return to Time Travel (2000)

Part Eight
A Wounded Healer (1995 to present)

Part One

Time Travel in the New Millennium (2000)

1. A Wax-flower Tree and a Scrapheap

Like a wax-flower tree under a bell of Glass in the
paisley and gingham county of McHenry is
Woodstock: grand capital of mid-Victorianism in the
Midwest.

Orson Welles, 1934

Hestia, help me please, I am searching for home.
I returned to Woodstock, Illinois thirty years after
my high school graduation there, to visit the
Children's Home where I'd grown up. I wanted to
drive, instead of fly, so that I could prepare myself
emotionally over the natural gap of distance and time
it would take to travel the nearly 1,000 miles. I also
wanted to savor the experience of returning to the
scrapheap of society where I'd been dumped as a kid,
in the brand-new, paid-cash-for, car of my dreams,
an elegant, black E-320 Mercedes-Benz. Maybe vain
of me, I admit, but such moments occur rarely in a
lifetime.

I wondered how I'd feel about being in Woodstock
and visiting the Home, from the perspective of my
new self and my new life. I wondered if strong emotions would overwhelm me, or if I'd just feel curious
about the history and local color of the town, as I do
when visiting a place I've read about, and for a long
time planned to visit. Maybe it would feel like visiting
my home in a past life, giving me a sense of *déjà vu.*

I would not be able to look anybody up. Even the
most casual conversations, with the Innkeeper, wait-
ers, or store clerks, would be awkward. I would have
to be careful about revealing too much of myself.
People would naturally try to place me, would ask

when I'd graduated from high school. Somebody would certainly be my age, or know someone who was. After a while, someone would surely ask around about this guy who drives into town in a conspicuous car bearing an out-of-state license plate, claiming to have been reared in the Children's Home of decades past, claiming to have attended three of the local public schools, and demonstrating astonishing knowledge about Woodstock, and the historic Children's Home. But of course, no one will have ever heard of me.

I knew there were a few persons still in the Woodstock area who had lived there when I did, including several kids from the Home, because I had kept in touch over the years by intermittently subscribing to the local newspaper. I knew that one of the Home boys had been elected mayor of Woodstock; and another Home guy was a local police sergeant. And I knew that my high school math teacher was still teaching and that he served on the city council.

When I lived in the Home, there had been this photojournalist gentleman in town; he'd also been on the Board of Directors of the Children's Home. Years later, I had commuted with his wife on the Chicago & Northwestern train into Chicago, where I finished my undergraduate degree at Roosevelt University and she was completing a graduate degree in psychology at Loyola University.

Now I knew that she'd completed her studies and had opened her private practice in family counseling according to her hopes and dreams, which she'd described to me during our train commutes of years ago. I would have liked to congratulate her for bringing her dreams to fruition and to let her know that I had also happily survived my life so far. But of course I couldn't, at least not without some preliminary explaining.

3

I knew that her husband was still writing articles and taking photographs throughout McHenry County, and that he still ran his business out of the same house. I called him once long distance in a nostalgic mood just to order his calendar of historical photographs called "Memorable Moments in Woodstock." One thing led to another in the easy flowing conversation, but I ended the call when he started asking me if I knew this person or that person; and all he named, I knew. He was trying to place me of course. He was polite and affable with just an edge of journalistic curiosity, but that was his nature, and exactly as I'd remembered him to be.

How entertaining it would be to reminisce about Woodstock and about living in the Home in the sixties, to find out what happened to so many of the kids I've wondered about over the years, to get the gossip about the townsfolk of then and now, and to surreptitiously find out what, if anything, was known about me.

In anticipation of my trip I'd read everything I could find on Woodstock, but I was disappointed to find no mention of the historical Children's Home which had operated continuously for over seventy-five years, on Woodstock's website, or in any other public relations or Chamber of Commerce literature.

Both the former Home-boy mayor and the photojournalist could easily be called Mr. Woodstock in that each could no doubt provide me with a satiating amount of historical detail about Woodstock events and residents. I imagined the many hours we could spend reminiscing. But like Homer's Odysseus, I needed to return home in disguise; for me a type of double disguise. For both Odysseus and me, it was a disguise which was nearly unbearable.

I wondered what had happened to Mike Stompanato, who owned the barbershop on Main

Street across from the movie theatre. Mike was the cousin of Johnny Stompanato, ex-bodyguard of gangster Mickey Cohen, who was killed in 1958 by Lana Turner's then-fourteen-year-old daughter, Cheryl Crane.

When I lived in the Home there was always this innuendo that Mike Stompanato and a local physician, Paul C. Johnson, were in some sort of dubious cahoots. Maybe it was all childhood imaginings, but Dr. Johnson sure was an oddball guy, with shifty eyes and a nervous, twitchy demeanor; he'd never married and was a loner. And the notion that he and Stompanato, who even in his white barber's uniform had a worldly air about him, could be associated in any way was so unlikely that it must have been true.

Dr. Johnson was the Children's Home physician, and a couple of us Home kids, including me, had worked for both Stompanato and his wife doing various odd jobs around the barbershop and at their home. So we had opportunity to observe them and fuel our imaginations, but that was all there was to it because none of us ever discovered anything really scandalous about them.

**

So I was traveling back to Chicago and Woodstock, Illinois, after having transcended my childhood there. I'm in excellent health, married, and by all appearances just a regular guy. I'm a Physician's Associate on medical staff at Duke University Medical Center. I have been called a country club Republican; I guess I could have turned out worse. I'm aware that I give the appearance of having been born into male privilege, born with a silver spoon in my mouth. Appearing much younger than

5

my age, it's erroneously assumed that I've had an easy life. None of that is true.

I have not had an easy life, I was not born into privilege and I was not born male.

There. Now, it took me just a few moments to say that and how glib it all sounds to me; but in no amount of time could I figure out, much less explain how I've made it to this point in my life. Nevertheless, I must try.

***

After traveling west from Chicago for about an hour on the clamorous, truck driven Interstate 80, I finally came to state Route 47. Coming off the interstate onto the broadly curving exit ramp, I was immediately soothed by the uncluttered, expansive farm fields. Then turning north and traveling toward Woodstock, I passed by tidy farms on both sides of the highway, each with its sentinel silo. No junk cars decomposing in the driveways, no junk couches slouching on the front porch, no plastic flamingos or any other clutter on the properties, and not a scrap of liter along the road.

Woodstock, the county seat of McHenry County, is a small town with plenty of pinochle players. It has managed over the years not only to retain, but to enhance and capitalize upon its inherent Victorian charm and "All American City" (1964) character. The town is built around a square and this entire downtown area is on the National Register of Historic Places.

The two-acre Park-in-the-Square is the center of town, and is bulk-headed to the broad, brick road flowing around it. In the park are mature oak trees and several statues of war veterans. From 1955 to

6

1974, the VFW sponsored the annual VJ Day parades, which featured several of the region's Drum & Bugle Corps; my favorite was the Madison Scouts, an all-male corps still in existence today.

The Opera House, occupying the south end of the square and facing north, was built in 1889 and has been used continuously since. It was used for Chicago's first summer stock theatre. Roger Hill, headmaster of Woodstock's Todd School for Boys, produced Shakespeare plays starring his student Orson Welles, and staged them at the Opera House in 1934.

The Todd Seminary for Boys, as it was originally named, was a progressive private school founded in 1873 by The Reverend Richard K. Todd, a Presbyterian minister. In the early 1920's a record-ed enrollment was 110 boys, coming from seventeen states and territories. Todd School's most notable graduate was Orson Welles, who came to the School at age nine from Kenosha, Wisconsin. The school was closed in 1954.

The Courthouse was built in 1857 and occupies the west side of the square. Now privately owned, it houses the local Arts Council and the Dick Tracy Museum. Chester Gould, creator of the Dick Tracy comic strip in 1931, made his home in the Bull Valley area of Woodstock. "Dick Tracy Days" is an annual festival on the square and culminates in a traditional Woodstock Drum & Bugle Corps pageant.

The jail was added to the Courthouse in 1887 and is now the "Jailhouse," an upscale pub where diners may be seated in one of the original cell blocks and feast on such menu selections as the "Burger-Ler" or the "Steakout Sandwich."

Just a short walk northwest of the square is the same Dairy Queen where we bought ice cream cones and Dilly Bars on our walk home from Olson Junior

High school.

Before reaching the Dairy Queen, we'd pass by St. Mary's Catholic Church. The huge, heavy wooden front doors were always unlocked. Sometimes after school I sneaked into this other world. The silent sanctuary, with its stained glass windows depicting Bible stories and other meditative scenarios, extended upwards to high, convex ceilings and was cool and dark. There was a lingering sweet fragrance of incense. At the front, to the left of the altar, a candle shimmering in a translucent red lantern was suspended from the ceiling by a chain, a vigil light, and a sign to worshippers that the Blessed Sacrament was there on reserve. Many small votive candles flickered in a wrought-iron rack at the back of the church. It was so utterly quiet and serene that the sound of my footsteps seemed amplified as I crept down the center aisle, daring to approach the altar. The altar was dressed in several layers of red and white fine linens and seemed regal with its stately brass candelabras. The baptismal font placed at the back of the sanctuary symbolizing a Christian's entry into the church, the marble icons, the statues, paintings and portraits of Mary and of the crucifixion of Jesus, were fascinating, mystical, and compelling to me.

***

Woodstock, Illinois, not Punxsutawney, Pennsylvania, is where Columbia Pictures' "Groundhog Day" was filmed in 1992, and the town has since celebrated this event annually. The tavern scene in the movie was filmed in Woodstock's "Jailhouse" pub. The Cherry Street Inn, which was the Bed & Breakfast in the movie, is really a private home on South Madison Street. And the Pennsylvania Hotel interiors depicted in the movie were filmed inside Woodstock's famous Opera House on the square. The bowling scene was filmed at Wayne's Lanes, still on East Church Street, and the dance was filmed at the Moose Lodge on Clay Street. Both Wayne's Lanes and the Moose Lodge were on the route we walked to school when I lived at the Home in the sixties.

***

I knew that the Children's Home, as it had operated when I lived there and before, no longer existed. It had been closed just a couple of years after I was graduated from high school. The main building of the Children's Home, which had been at 840 North Seminary Avenue since March 19, 1891 when the Chicago Industrial Home for Children moved to Woodstock, was torn down in 1983 to make way for a $4.5 million senior citizens' complex, to include the existing retirement home Sunset Manor, which was renamed Carefree Village as it is known today.

When I was fifteen years old in 1967, I went to work at Sunset Manor as a nursing assistant, my first payroll job. I had been regularly employed in many non-payroll jobs before that. I was paid $0.75 per hour and was raised to $1.00 per hour after a couple of months. (Minimum wage in February 1967 was $1.40, and in February 1968 it was raised to $1.60, then raised to $2.00 in May 1974) With the exception of two years, one while in medical training doing my clinical rotations when I actually paid tuition to work full-time, I've paid into social security and income taxes every year since 1967.

My work at Sunset Manor in the skilled nursing

unit was physically demanding and many times emotionally draining. All patients I cared for were bedbound, total lift and total care. I used a hammock-like, hydraulic pump-operated lift (which we still use in the DUMC dialysis unit today) to move the patients from the bed to a chair. In the winter of 1968 there was a pneumonia epidemic and six or eight of my patients died from pneumonia, including Mr. and Mrs. Coates and Mrs. Outen.

The old Harrison House building, where the Children's Home teenagers lived, is situated just south of the Main Building. The Harrison House building, as it was renamed in honor of its benefactor, was purchased from the Todd School when it closed in 1954. The building was known as Grace Hall, when owned by the Todd School.

The old Harrison House building was not torn down when the main building of the Children's Home was razed in February 1983; and with the exception of some interior remodeling, it remains the same. It is now called Christian Life Care, and is now used as administrative offices for a children's day care center.

Adjacent to the old Harrison House building is the only other extant building of the Todd School for Boys campus. This building is now the privately owned Rogers Hall Apartments.

I traveled north on Seminary Avenue from the five-way intersection and approached the seventeen-acre campus of the Children's Home along the right side of the road. Though it was thirty-eight years ago, I can easily remember the first day I came to the Woodstock Children's Home.

Part Two

The Woodstock Children's Home
(1963-1970)

2. The Little Lad and the Odyssey

When my father and my mother forsake me, then
the Lord will take me up.
Psalms 27:10

The day was March 28, 1963; just several months
after the Cuban Missile Crisis. My younger sister
Esther and I rode the CTA bus with my parents to the
Department of Child & Family Services, in Chicago.
We got off the bus and crossed a large intersection.
The vision of an imposing brick and concrete build-
ing across the broad street still looms in my memory.

My sister and I had first been made wards of the
state in 1954, when I was two years old, and had been
placed in foster care at that time. But on this day,
we were going to the DCFS to be processed and then
immediately taken to the Woodstock Children's
Home, where we stayed until high school graduation.

Inside, the building was austere and forbidding,
with concrete walls and slate and marble floors. The
dark wood furniture was bare of upholstery, and the
sound of scraping chairs echoed ominously throughout those cavernous rooms with high ceilings.
Esther and I were shuttled from one dizzying processing station to another where various school and
health information was collected and recorded. I was
about to burst out of my skin with fear and anxiety;
and each successive encounter with the kind but
impersonal social workers and other various bureaucrats escalated my already acute insecurity and fear
of the unknown.

The last processing station was for a physical
exam. Here the disrobing and the overpowering

12

manner of the examiners terrified me. Then the phlebotomist, in a casual manner proceeded to draw blood from the inside of my elbow. She and I sat silently and watched as the bluish-red blood slowly filled the glass tube. Each subsequent tube seem to take longer and longer to fill, and it occurred to me that there was a limit to the blood she could draw out of me. After each tube was filled, she slowly twisted it off the long, large-bore needle which she'd used to cannulate my vein, and then replaced it with another, and yet another bottomless tube. She did this with deliberate ritualism, eyeing me coolly and surreptitiously. She seemed to take pleasure in this slow exsanguination of my blood. I wondered, *how much more, how much more?*

I had to will myself to sit still; I was terrorized but didn't dare say a word, having learned from earliest memory that the slightest sound or movement out of me, even a cry of terror, would result in my father's fist in my face.

After an eternity passed and four tubes of blood, each with a different color cap, lie on the table next to my arm, I felt myself break out in a cold sweat and begin to shiver. Then my ears began to roar; the room dimmed and flickered, and then everything in front of me went black. When I regained consciousness, my shirt clung to me in cold wet sweat and my hair was damp. I was lying on a cot and a nurse was coaxing me to drink orange juice. It was cold and refreshing and I was hungry. As usual, we hadn't eaten yet that day though it was about noon. The kind ladies eventually reassured me that we had completed our processing work with the DCFS and were soon to be on our way to our new home in Woodstock.

I was greatly relieved to get out of that dark, horrible building. We were taken to the Children's Home

13

by a cheerful and energetic social worker, named Eleanor Hall, no relation to us. She wore a flowered cotton dress with a sash around her waist that flattered her full figure. She had fair skin and red hair which was apparently very long. It was braided into fat coils that were wrapped around the back of her head and pinned into place. She put us in a tan Volkswagen beetle. My sister and I had no bags, no luggage, absolutely no belongings at all, and so it was an easy fit.

It was fun to ride in that spiffy little car; I sat in the front seat and watched in amazement as the sprite social worker drove, shifting through the gears, working the pedals. She wore dark brown leather sandals, with open toes, open heels and no stockings. She had freckles apparently over every inch of her body including the tops of her feet and toes. She both drove that car and talked a mile a minute, her arms, feet, and her head and mouth all moving at the same time. I had never seen my father behind the wheel of a car; he couldn't get a drivers' license because of his severe epilepsy and he couldn't have ever afforded a car anyway. The only car I'd ridden in was my grandfather's large sedan, and so all this was new and fun. Esther soon fell asleep in the back seat.

After we rode about sixty minutes northwest of the city, the scenery became idyllic with expanses of green fields, mature trees and plenty of corn fields. The corn rows were planted perpendicular to the highway and were hypnotic as I tried to focus on them going by: zip, zip, zip, through my window. When we got to McHenry County, herds of grazing, black and white Holstein cows were frequent, dotting the pastures. I was more relaxed by this time.

After awhile, she asked if we were hungry. I was always hungry and had been for as long as I could remember. She put on her left turn signal, down-shifted, stopped and fidgeted while waiting for oncoming traffic to pass. And then we roared into the McDonald's parking lot in Crystal Lake. With a flick of her wrist, she turned off the ignition key, from which hung a long leather strap; and the little bug sputtered and shuddered and seemed to roll over dead.

She assured us in her animated way that we were sure to like this food. She chatted on, saying that the first McDonald's franchise had been built in nearby Des Plaines, in 1955. She bought us each a hamburger, French fries, and a chocolate milkshake. We sat outside and ate; the air was cool but the sun was warm. I'd never eaten McDonald's food before and it was indescribably delicious.

The next town northwest on Route 14 was Woodstock. Upon approaching, we saw a large green road sign:

> "Welcome to Woodstock, no radar, no timers. We don't rely on gadgets. We count on you. Drive safely."

This same welcome sign, I learned later, was posted at each major highway that led into town.

We arrived at the Home about 4:15 p.m. The kids were just getting home from school. All kids at the Home attended public schools. As a matter of fact, this was the foremost requirement: if for any reason a child could not attend public school, then he could not live at the Woodstock Children's Home.

My sister and I were brought to the administration offices at the main building to be checked in. Even before we got up to the dorms, the first kid I met was Carol. She was friendly and cheerful; and I was grateful for that. She had a shapely, delicate fig-

15

ure and full breasts. Even though she was two years older than me, I was taller and heavier.

She wanted to show me around and took me outside. Along the north side of the building was a merry-go-round, which had a flat platform and was divided into eighths, like a pie, by metal handlebars. The idea was that you needed several kids to get on it at the same time for optimal fun. You stood inside the merry-go-round on the platform, on your right leg, and with your left leg on the ground. Then, like riding a scooter, each kid pushed off from the ground, getting it to go around and around, faster and faster, in a clockwise direction.

A softball field lay behind the main building, at the east end of the property, and a swing-set was nearby. Carol and I got the idea for both of us to get on one of the swings standing up, facing each other. She put her feet between mine on the small wooden seat; my feet were flush against the inside of the seat frame and my legs rubbed against the chains.

Then we figured out how to get the swing going. I would pump my legs moving the swing forward, and then alternately she would pump, moving the swing in the opposite direction. After a short time, we got that swing flying so high that when it was my turn to push off, I was looking straight up at the sky, and when it was her turn, I was staring face down at the grass below.

At the same time that the swing was flying me to its backward crest on her pumping cycle, my knees would be slowly bending, until they were completely hyperflexed and the swing seat was just inches from my rear end. Then at just the moment that I could feel the swing was going to change directions, I would push off as hard as I could. And turning my face up to the sky, I'd relax while she then picked up the rhythm.

16

Whenever we'd fly the swing just slightly higher than parallel to the ground, it would lose centrifugal force and the chains would go slack and we'd seem to be falling to the ground. But then after a few free falling seconds, the chains would jerk tight again and we'd feel the small wooden seat firmly against the bottom of our feet.

When it was her turn to be butt up and facing the ground, she would howl with glee; and laughing, her elbows would collapse and her soft, slight body would crash into me, but we held tightly onto the chains, laughing all the while. And when the slack chains snapped taut, and caught up with our pumping legs, we were flying high again, heading back up around to the other side.

3. Learning the Rules of the Road

With the exception of the softball field and swing set, the Home didn't have any indoor or outdoor play facilities; and so the house parents were always driving us kids somewhere, all loaded up in one of the aqua and beige colored Volkswagen microbuses.

Occasionally on a Saturday, we'd talk them into driving us up to Lake Geneva, Wisconsin. We filled a large cardboard box with lunches packed in brown paper bags and we made a day of it. Nothing imaginable to us kids could have been more fun than a day at the lake.

During the summers, grade school kids attended Vacation Bible School at the nearby Free Methodist Church; and we went to the McHenry County Fair each July. We spent as much time as we could at the municipal pool, which is still at what is now called Emricson Park. We got "unlimited swimming" passes and with fumbling fingers, I sewed the one by two inch rectangular patch onto the bottom right edge of my swim suits. We seemed never to tire of swimming and begged the house parents every day to drive us to the city pool, which was on the opposite outskirts of town more than five miles away.

***

Even by the time I went to live at the Home, I was already quite a swimmer. Without any formal instruction, I had worked my way through the Red Cross proficiency tests to the level of junior lifesaver.

At age five, while living with my parents, I got special permission to attend Chicago's Moody Memorial

19

Church summer camp at Loon Lake, Wisconsin, and went every summer thereafter until we were placed in the Home. I went to camp on a "scholarship," as my parents could not afford to pay my way. Each year, I had to memorize and recite Bible passages and the order of the books of the Bible to my Sunday school teachers, in order to qualify to attend summer camp. I went alone without my sister.

I thrived in summer camp: we swam a couple of times a day, played outside team sports, and had arts & crafts classes. Every morning we woke up to the sound of a bugle; and before breakfast I heard the sound of many screen doors slamming as we bounded out of our cabins. Herding ourselves towards the field in front of the campground, we lined up in squads facing the flag-pole and the leader. He led us in a vigorous exercise session, which included jumping jacks, touching the toes, push ups, and other exercises, ending with a run around the field. We raised the flag in the morning and returned to our squads before supper to ceremoniously lower the flag and then fold it in lengthwise thirds, then in triangles, ending in one stuffed, pillow-like triangle.

We ate in a large noisy dining room at long wooden tables and benches. We ate huge meals; breakfast included pancakes, eggs, sausage, milk, toast, juice, cereal. For lunch we ate barbequed beef sandwiches, hamburgers, and hot dogs. For supper we ate meatloaf, chicken, hearty stews and casseroles, green beans, tomatoes, corn on the cob, peach cobbler and ice cream. Then we had snacks at the canteen in the evening.

Before bed each night, we had vespers around the campfire at the lakeside. One of the counselors always had a guitar and led us in gospel songs and Bible reading. After dark the crickets bleated incessantly. We were tired as we stumbled back up the hill to our cabins and our bunk beds.

At the end of the week there was an awards ceremony. I won awards in swimming, running, and arts & crafts. I never got homesick to return to my parents in Chicago.

***

But for summer memories, nothing could top Riverview. How do kids today live without Riverview? Riverview was Chicago's famous amusement park of days past, located at Western and Belmont Avenues. It opened on July 2, 1904, and closed after the season, on September 4, 1967. The Pair-O-Chutes, the Blue Streak, the Bobs, and the Fireball were a just a few of the many roller coaster rides and attractions.

I had even been to Riverview once with my father before Esther and I were placed in the Children's Home. Even though I was younger than the minimum age limit to ride it, we rode the Fireball together because it was the fastest and steepest roller coaster ride at the time.

We were secured in with only a leather strap across our laps; and it seemed I couldn't push hard enough against the metal bar in front of us to hold myself in my seat. As we crept up the steep tracks, over the mechanical roar and passenger screams, my father yelled as loudly as he could, "When we go downhill, hold the bar tightly, lock your elbows, and push hard, like this" and he demonstrated his locked elbows to me. But when the going got rough, he wrapped his right arm tightly around my middle and hung onto the bar with his left hand as the open-top, red cars jerked and we were whipped around the curves. He held onto me, as from the top we were hurled face down the tracks, toward the ground.

21

Later, the Children's Home bused us into Riverview several times when we were kids. And then I went again as a high school student, with older kids who'd gotten permission to drive from Woodstock into Chicago. Riverview was great fun for kids of all ages.

***

During the winter, our favorite activity was roller skating. We Home kids piled into the buses and the house parents dutifully drove us to the roller skating rinks, in McHenry or Crystal Lake, where we skated countless counterclockwise laps around and around. In high school we discovered the Chicago Hub and The Elm in Elmhurst. In those days, live organists entertained us from a loft above the rink, up from where the light show came. The organ was so loud and with so much bass that you could feel the vibrations and resonance in your chest and ears long after the music stopped. I can still see the organist up in the loft, his left foot bouncing all over the bass pedal. There were "swell shades" on the ceiling, flaps that would blow open when loud volume was applied using the organ's large foot pedal.

There was a floor guard, always with a whistle in his teeth, and on which he had a low threshold to blast. During intermission, he'd go out on the empty floor, and skating backwards, he'd bang two large canisters together, with perforated tops like huge salt shakers, distributing copious amounts of rosin onto the floor. This was to give us better purchase on the floor as we cut the deep inside and outside edges of our skating dance patterns.

In the darkened rinks, during the special dance numbers like the waltz, the rosin made swirling,

22

ethereal dust clouds in the white lights flickering and sweeping overhead, making even the most modestly talented couple look romantic and glamorous, or at least feel that way. At the end of the evening we were sticky with sweat because the rosin dust made our hair gummy and our skin tacky. There was no air conditioning in those days, so we tended mostly to go roller skating in the winter.

We would use a skate wrench to loosen our trucks, the trucks being the front axle of the skate. Then while skating, as you applied pressure with your forefoot to either the inside or outside front wheels, the axle would give, displacing the wheel downward, making it easier to cut deep edges, and making it easier to lean into the graceful arcs you'd trace on the floor.

To cut a forward inside edge, for example, with loosened trucks, would take just a small amount of pressure on the medial aspect of your big toe. For an outside edge, you'd lean outward, pressing slightly along the lateral aspect of the foot. Too much pressure on too loose a truck and you'd fall flat on your face.

With the other end of the skate wrench, we'd remove and rotate the wheels. With all the edging, mostly inside edging, the wheels would wear just like a tire. And so to keep this wheel wear even and also just to look cool, we were constantly rotating our wheels and adjusting our trucks.

***

Other times, house parents would load us into the Home's beige and aqua colored Volkswagen microbuses, and in just a short time we could be out of the cow pastures and corn fields, and after a raucous ride, we'd be rolling into the parking lot of Chicago's awesome Museum of Science and Industry.

After a dizzying morning, walking into each other, distracted by such visual over-stimulation as the many nations' colorful flags hanging over a high balcony just inside the larger-than-life front entrance, and such exciting exhibits as the coal mine, the submarine, the whispering gallery, the prenatal fetuses, and the space capsule, the house parents would pass out our lunches pulled from a large cardboard box, which were in brown paper bags splotched with grease from the peanut butter and jelly sandwiches inside.

***

We also went sledding at Veterans Acres in nearby Crystal Lake, where there was a perfect sledding hill. Along with many other children, we trudged up that hill, and then polished it to a pearly, icy finish by going down countless many times with our sleds or plastic saucers.

Behind the Harrison House was a field. House parent Mr. Beatty let us tie sleds to the back of his old red Ford pickup truck, and he pulled us around the field and through the unplowed side streets. After doing that for a couple of hours, we'd trundle in through the basement, where the kitchen was, to make hot cocoa and snacks.

Friday nights, if we didn't go to the gym at the local Illinois National Guard Armory on Madison Street, we were allowed to watch television. We had "party night" and the house parents would allow us an unbelievably free rein in the kitchen. With Chicago radio station WLS blasting rock and roll from our ubiquitous transistor radios; we'd make popcorn, caramel corn, chocolate fudge, cookies, or cakes. We were allowed to make whatever we wanted, as long as we cleaned up after ourselves.

The kitchen was equipped with large stoves, huge cooking pots and pans. There was a dishwashing room with a four-stage assembly line process. We had an enormous walk-in freezer, and it's a wonder that no one ever got trapped in it with all the horsing around that went on during our party nights.

We watched the old classic movies on Friday nights, and gorged on sweets. Someone had an electric guitar and we plugged it into an old amplifier housed in a wooden case. I never got tired of strumming through the arpeggio chords of the gritty Animals', "House of The Rising Sun." There was an old honky-tonk sounding piano in the living room which a couple of us liked to play and we spent hours picking out tunes by ear. I taught myself to read music and play from hymn books. Many of us could sing and could make music, though of dubious quality. With the exception of enjoying our music, the house parents seemed to have as much fun as we did on these Friday party nights.

In the earlier days, there was a Children's Home choir, directed by Rosalie Gearheart. She was proud of her choir and she really fawned over all twenty or so of us. We all wore white shirts, the girls wore black cotton skirts gathered at the waist, handmade by Mrs. Robinson; and the boys wore black trousers from Montgomery Ward's.

We all wore bow ties made of black grosgrain ribbon, and Mrs. Gearheart was constantly fussing over our ties and our hair.

She had flashing brown eyes, dark brown, thick, wavy hair, and she always wore deep red lipstick on her full mouth. She had a soft, voluptuous figure and always smelled good; she was so pretty and we did our best to please her with our singing. We traveled in the microbuses to various regional Free Methodist churches and performed at their Sunday-night services. The church groups always fed us heartily and seem to genuinely enjoy us and our singing.

***

We weren't allowed to go to the movies; it was against the rules of the Home, but one time the Gearhearts took us anyway, to see *Mary Poppins* at a nearby movie theatre. None of us little kids had ever been inside a movie theatre; I certainly hadn't. We all .sat together in a long row, munching the popcorn they bought for us. Mr. and Mrs. Gearheart, a young, attractive couple with plenty of chemistry between them, sat in the row behind us. When the movie was over, she like an excited child said she enjoyed it so much that she wanted to sit through it again. She asked us if we wanted to too, and of course we did.

I made the cheerleading squad in the seventh grade, but I couldn't attend the dances, as going to dances was against the Home's rules. Dancing or even just attending a dance, including the Prom, was utterly forbidden by the Home.

In order to attend my eighth grade graduation, I was asked to sign a contract written by the Executive Director himself, saying that I could attend and participate in all the activities except the dance. The graduation dance was the biggest social event of all in our young lives and the most fun. School dances were very popular events, and if you were anyone in this small town of Woodstock, you attended. They were excellent, well chaperoned, non-threatening venues for kids to learn social skills and how to inter-

26

act with the opposite sex. Not being allowed to attend school dances, which were always associated with other important socializing events such as formal dinners or school football and basketball games, was a huge social deprivation, causing me to retreat from my teenage life. I was intelligent and well-liked, and I could have easily taken on class leadership roles. But class leaders were highly visible and would be expected to attend the school dances and other social events.

I refused to sign, contending that the evil of high school dances, beheld by the executive director, was in his mind, not in mine or anyone else's. Furthermore, I resented him projecting his "dirty mind" onto me. My kind of independent thinking infuriated him and the house parents.

I had transportation difficulties getting to the games to cheer, and I also had schedule conflicts with my after-school and weekend jobs. I was stunned that I made the squad, which was achieved by auditioning twice—first in front of the faculty, and then for the student body; but I was athletic, coordinated, and had a high jump. No one from the Home seemed the least bit interested that I had made the squad, no one congratulated me, and no one helped to get me to the games.

I was continuously anxious about trying to hide my Home-kid status from the rest of the squad and my classmates. In addition to lacking support from the Home, I had low self-esteem, so even though I was athletic and intelligent, I soon learned to avoid excelling in anything so as not to call attention to myself and my inferior status. I was humiliated to be a ward of the state and a resident of the Children's Home in this middle to upper-middle class town. Woodstock seemed very high class indeed compared to the rat-roach-infested slums of Chicago where I'd most recently lived with my parents before coming to the Children's Home.

To those who, upon discovering that I lived at the Home, would always ask why, I found it painful to answer that my parents were not dead; or that my father was not an alcoholic or anything like that. He was a Methodist minister, as it says on my original birth certificate, with an appointment in Ohio. He was the son of a prominent, life-long Methodist minister and three-term Ohio State Representative.

Similarly, my mother's father, Ora Hampton Harrop, had ample resources and left an inheritance to all ten of his children.

And no, I couldn't explain how my father remained employed and married to my mother while Esther and I stayed in the Home. How after his father died, he abandoned my mother after putting her in Elgin State Mental Hospital, and ran off to Tennessee with my two younger brothers. How he then divorced my mother in the mental hospital, from out–of–state and then remarried a woman with three school-aged children of her own. How he could get away with all this, without any accountability, even to this day.

It looked to my school friends like there just was not any good explanation for why I was a ward of the state and a Home kid, such as that my parents were killed in Africa while doing missionary work or something noble like that. I always wished I could say that my parents had died some honorable death, but that wasn't the truth. And so then, not seeing any obvious default of my parents as the reason for my being in the Home, people sometimes assumed that I was there because of some fault of my own.

It was furthermore unexplainable how, after my father had neatly gotten rid of Esther and me, he and my mother managed to have, after her 1959 miscarriage, two more children, my brothers, Lawrence

Melvin and Phillip Webster, eight and ten years younger than I. He adamantly insisted that "his boys" stay with him, even though he placed them in a nearby Children's Home in Tennessee, as soon as he arrived there.

As soon as he could, he conned another woman into marrying him and then immediately got my younger brothers out of the Children's Home to live with him, his new wife, and her three children, in her house. He got his ready-made family in Tennessee and told no one that he left Esther and me in the Children's Home, and a wife in the State Mental Hospital, back in Illinois.

So I didn't try out for cheerleading the following year or try out for anything in high school, either. I tried to stay invisible and literally counted down the days until I could get out of the Home.

***

I spent my school days hoping to hide the fact that I was a Home kid. I lived in constant dread that anyone would find out. Amazingly, since I was a good student, it was never suspected by my classmates and teachers. Almost no one knew, or if they did, they didn't seem to let on to me, except for this one occasion. And so for that reason, even though I was well-liked and respected by my classmates, I kept to myself, retreating from life. Living in shame constrained me from developing healthy relationships, and from living up to my fullest potential.

In the Home, we had to attend study hall for ninety minutes each school evening. For most kids, it was just an agony to be endured. We were just putting in time; and no real effort to actually tutor, mentor, or even attend to school work was put forth by the noncollege-educated house parents. The most important thing to them was that we put in our time, even if we did nothing. Just as no one gave a word of praise to those of us who did well in school, neither did they say anything to the kids who flunked classes. Those kids were just passed along and they certainly were not flunked out of school for academic reasons.

The attitude towards kids like me who did well in school went something like this: "Oh good, you're so smart; we don't have to worry about you. Now help us take care of these other kids."

No teacher or house parent ever said a word of encouragement to me about planning for college. When the time came for all of that, I did all the applications myself. After much banging of my head against the wall, I found out how to apply for financial aid. To this day, I can't imagine where I got the moxie to apply to college and for financial aid, much less the resolve and perseverance to finish.

One evening, my high school math teacher filled in for the house parent during our required evening study hall. This was unusual, as teachers from the schools were not hired to run the study halls; perhaps if they had been, the time might have been more profitably spent. When he walked into the basement of the Harrison House, where we had study hall around the large table in the mess hall, we both were shocked to see each other. He in no way tried to conceal his surprise at seeing me there.

"Do *you* live here?" he exclaimed with deliberate indiscreetness.

I was mortified. My suspicion as to what the teachers thought about the Home kids was confirmed in that split-second. They thought that any kid from the Home couldn't possibly be a good student. I had gotten a final grade of "B" in his class with no great effort; I simply paid attention. I sat in front row so I wouldn't miss a thing and ate up every word of the class lectures. I guess he just couldn't believe that one of his better students was one of "those Home kids."

***

Mr. Leeds was an unlikely houseparent for teenagers living at the Harrison House. He alternated with Mr. and Mrs. Beatty, who lived in the tiny staff quarters there. Mr. Leeds, always with his cup of coffee in his hand and his clipboard of notes nearby, was a retired military officer. He once cheerfully told me that he'd served in three branches of the United States military. He was robust and energetic; he lived with his frail, pretty but sickly-appearing wife in the staff housing just east of the main building. They had no children and their marriage seemed strained, with a sad pallor to it. The marriage seemed to be something they each endeavored to endure with stoicism and grace. Mr. Leeds was very squared away, but he had a heart, possibly to a fault. He was always his own man, not overly religious like the other house parents were, and he was always a gentleman.

One Saturday afternoon, on his day off, he had planned to take a carload of teenagers from the Harrison House out riding around. At the last minute, all the kids, except me, declined or had other things to do, and so he asked if I still wanted to go. I told him sure, and so he picked me up in his 1963 Rambler with the three-speed shift under the steering wheel. We drove up to Lake Geneva, Wisconsin, and all over the surrounding resort area, as so many people did on Sunday afternoons. "Riding around" was the primary leisure activity for kids and adults of all ages when I was growing up in the Midwest.

We stopped at a cheese outlet and he bought a hunk of sharp cheddar cheese, some crackers, and cokes. Outside we perched on the top of a picnic table; he sliced the cheese with his pocket knife and we sat eating, watching the endless stream of sightseeing cars go by.

On the drive back to Woodstock, we came through some country roads instead of the main highway Route 47. On one deserted straightaway, he let the car roll to a stop. Then he let the gear shift gently flop into neutral position, and stomped on the ratchet-sounding emergency brake with his left foot.

"Okay," he said with feigned seriousness, "I'm tired of driving; now it's your turn," and he rolled out the door. Walking around the back of the car, he slapped the trunk lid with his left hand, and called out, "Alright, let's go."

I slid over, the seat was warm. He jumped in and fumbled for the seat release latch on the door side with his right hand. He told me to find the same latch on my door side, with my left hand. On the count of three, we each released our latches and scooted the bench seat forward so that my feet could reach the pedals.

Then I engaged the clutch, put my foot on the brake, released the emergency brake, pulled the gear shift toward me and downward, and then I let my foot off the brake and tried to find the gas pedal.

Soon I learned that universal truth: one always needs to let up more on the clutch pedal, and give it less on the gas pedal than one is inclined to do. Off we went, the engine stuttering and the car rocking and lurching down the road. Though I'd watched him countless times, engaging the clutch pedal while at the same time pushing the gear shift up and away from me into second gear required my utmost concentration in order to keep the movements coordinated.

Mr. Leeds sat alertly but relaxed with his arms crossed in front of him and in a fatherly tone of voice, said repeatedly, "Keep your eyes on the road; don't look down at your hands; no need to look at the dashboard. Don't forget to keep your eyes on the road." The gear shift slid straight down easily into third gear and we were rolling past quiet cornfields on both sides. I was driving the car!

***

I took drivers' education in school as soon as I could and got a learner's permit at age fourteen. Before we could enroll in "behind-the wheel-training," we had to pass a semester-long classroom course in driver's education. The class was taught by Coach Bradley; I thought it all interesting and very much enjoyed the class. In addition to learning "the rules of the road," we learned many practical things, such as all the parts of the engine and their functions, basic engine mechanics, and maintenance.

They also showed us several gory, reel-to-reel movies, produced in connection with the Department of Motor Vehicles, which depicted in uncensored detail, including decapitated and dismembered bodies, numerous car accident scenes, one after another, and another and another. This was intended to have a sobering, deterring effect, and it certainly did on me.

I took my "behind-the-wheel" during the winter. The "student driver" cars were courtesy of Benoy Motors. Coach Bradley sat in the shotgun seat; all he had was a brake pedal on his side of the floor and a booming voice as his instructional tools, but that was all he needed. There were always three students in the car; one driving and two in the back seat who snickered at every mistake the student driver made.

Coach Bradley used the opportunity of the winter-semester classes to provide experience in winter driving; and he'd direct us to drive on back streets that had an uphill or downhill incline.

One time I was cautiously inching along a snow-packed, downhill road. In the rear view mirror, I glanced at the students in the back seat; they were quiet and looked pretty serious. Suddenly and with no provocation, Coach Bradley trounced on his brake pedal with a loud thump and the car slid mercilessly out of control.

Then he bellowed at me, "Don't hit the brakes; turn the wheel in the direction of the spin."

My mind was spinning too. *What in the hell did he do that for?* I had to think for a second, *Is it the front end or the back end of the car that's sliding? And which way was it sliding?*

Steering seemed useless and the power steering made the front wheels feel as though they were riding no more than a millimeter above the ice-glazed snow, just skimming crazily.

"Not so much. Don't oversteer," he bellowed. It was hard to avoid jerking the wheel around because he'd scared the shit out of me by tromping on the brake and bellowing in my ear. Somehow I got the car under control though I doubt by any skill on my part; the car just lost momentum but luckily I managed to miss the ditches and mailboxes on both sides of the road.

Afterwards I thought, *Geez, I sure hope you thought that was fun.*

"Now," he said with great gravity, "remember how the seat of your pants feels when the car is spinning out of control.

Remember that feeling and don't you ever forget it."

***

Very shortly after I'd gotten my coveted driver's license on my first attempt at age sixteen, Mr. Leeds asked me one Saturday afternoon if I'd take his car and drive to a nearby hardware store to pick up something for him. He asked me this as though it was a huge favor, but I know he was just finding an occasion for me to practice driving. It wasn't really anything important that needed to be picked up on that particular day, as far as I could tell. And besides, he could have easily picked up the gadget himself.

I was sure proud that he trusted me with his late-model, shiny royal blue Dodge Cornet; it felt expansive and luxurious to me. However, my overly cautious manner and great concern not to damage his car outweighed any bit of joy I might have experienced in that ride; I sure as hell didn't want to wreck his car. That was the first time I drove a car alone as a licensed driver.

4. Home's Not Where the Windows are Barred

At any given time, we all had several chores assigned to us. All the cleaning in the home was done by us kids, including yard work and heavy indoor cleaning, such as the floors. We cleaned countless floors, stripping the wax, inch by inch, with a small scraper, wax that had probably been applied scores of years earlier by the boys who'd lived at the Harrison House when it was Grace Hall and part of the Todd School; and then we scrubbed the floors and applied new wax.

All the table setting, table serving, table clearing, dish washing, bathroom cleaning, room cleaning, yard work, and laundry, including doing our own ironing—absolutely everything was done by us kids.

It took a team of kids to do the dishes after each meal. This involved a preliminary scraping off, then stacking the dishes in approximately two-foot square, sturdy, basket-like trays, then spraying them off, then lining them up on the aluminum counter, and finally running each tray, one at a time, through the dishwasher, pulling up and down the "in" door, and the "out" door, before and after each dishwashing cycle.

After each tray of dishes and flatware was washed in scalding water, we'd open the "out" door, let the billowing steam clear, pull the tray out and move it ahead on the aluminum counter. Then another tray was put into the steaming hot dishwasher; we slammed the doors shut and the cycle started again.

After many trays were washed in that hot, steaming room, it was another kid's job to put all the dishes and flatware away just as soon as the dishes had cooled off enough so that he could handle them. We never saw a hired hand, maid, or domestic worker. All the work was done by us.

There was a laundry house behind the main building. It was the older boys' job to do the laundry. There were several large industrial-sized machines used to do the wash, including an extractor, a machine that did the job equivalent to the spin cycle on today's laundry machines.

One Saturday morning, when it was Bud's turn at laundry duty, he came crashing through the screen door of the main building, yelling in a low guttural growl. His right arm was hanging in a bloody mangled mess of sinews, muscle and broken bone. He was holding his right wrist with his left hand to keep the arm from tearing free and falling to the floor. His artery was shooting a pulsing arc of blood into the air.

He seemed mad with terror knowing that he should hold pressure on the life-spilling artery, but just as urgently, he needed to support the dangling forearm and hand; as it seemed surely to tear free from the bloody strands, if left unsupported.

By the time he reached us, he was pale with gray eyes, but miraculously conscious and on his feet. Mr. Leeds, our house parent, grabbed a linen dish towel and tied it tight and high above his elbow. Then several of us kids helped Mr. Leeds get Bud into the old Ford station wagon and he drove with unrestrained speed and intensity to the local hospital just above the high school, about five miles away from the Home. Bud was stabilized at the hospital then soon transferred into Chicago's Presbyterian St. Luke's Hospital. There he underwent several rounds of surgery to re-attach the arm.

I took the Chicago & Northwestern train into Chicago to visit him. There he lay for many weeks unable to move, his mid section protected under a transparent germ-proof tent, while flesh, which the surgeons had skinned off his flank and had attached to the lifeless arm, was expected to grow. It was a long shot and they tried for months to save the arm. Bud was nearly crazy with having to stay flat on his back, with his right arm attached surrealistically to his flank by skin that had been flayed from his side. After all their heroic efforts, the skin graft did not take and gas gangrene set in. His right arm was amputated above the elbow; he was fourteen years old.

Bud was a likable, easy-going kid with robust health. Of above average intelligence, he excelled in math. He had no parents, no family, and no siblings. Fortunately, Mr. Leeds immediately stepped in as his surrogate father, as he'd done for Willie and Bennie and others before. The Home made some feeble attempts at getting Bud "vocational rehabilitation," though with an above average IQ, he certainly had college potential. On high school graduation, he received a pittance of an insurance settlement—about $25,000.00.

Bud struggled to prove himself. The first job he applied for after his tragic accident was a job as a water softener sales representative. He was denied the job because the interviewer said that he wouldn't be able to lift the water softeners onto the back of the truck. Bud, who was pretty stout and muscular, demonstrated his defiance to the supervisor and hoisted the heavy water softener up from the ground with his non-dominant left arm, and had it on the back of the service truck in one smooth movement. He was hired on the spot. Bud was quickly promoted into bookkeeping and other business administrative duties; the water softener asshole was sure lucky to have Bud, as smart and persistent as he was.

***

At the main building where the younger children lived, they built a "solitary confinement" room upstairs. It was a closet of a room, no more than four by eight feet, with no lights and no plumbing. There was one-foot square window with bars across it. It faced the parking lot along the north side of the main building. There was nothing in the room except a mattress and a portable potty. Meals were passed through a slot in a formidable door with a large lock.

Shortly after Bud lost his right arm, they put him in that solitary confinement room for several days for some minor misbehaving; I don't even remember what it was. We kids stood out in the parking lot looking up at the window. The other kids called for Bud, trying to get his attention. He made monkey faces back at us. The kids laughed and joked; they egged him on and then cheered him. But when I saw his face peering at us through the bars, I was horrified. I didn't think anything was funny at all. I had a chilly feeling that this indignation would push Bud past his limit; that he would never get over this. I felt the Home had gone too far with the solitary confinement room.

Bud had a lot of anger and frustration which he'd squelched in the beginning in favor of trying to prove himself. Maybe he became resentful, and a sense of helplessness and anger overwhelmed him; but he soon developed some self-destructive behaviors which mostly took the form of fast and reckless driving. He wrecked a couple of cars owned by the forbearing Mr. Leeds.

He seemed to continue his downward spiral, later ending up in jail. Our twenty-year high school

40

reunion directory listed him as deceased.

***

Occasionally kids went AWOL from the Home. This was accomplished by going out the windows, onto the roof and then down the gutters or just jumping down into the bushes. It was not possible to simply walk out the doors at night because all the doors had alarms.

One night a group of teenage girls sneaked out of the Harrison House. I found out the next morning at the breakfast table. I had my own room and having worked hard at the Sunset Manor nursing home that evening, I slept soundly through the night. They went out a window at the end of the hallway of the girl's dorm, which conveniently opened out onto the carport roof of the house parents' main-level quarters.

When the house parents found out, all of those girls were sent to the doctor for "virginity tests." And then Mrs. Beatty announced the virginity status of each girl, as reported to her by Dr. Johnson, the Home's General Practitioner, to the entire group of Harrison House teenagers.

When confronted with the argument that a pregnancy couldn't be determined so soon after the alleged copulations, Mrs. Beatty readily admitted that the house parents didn't really care about that. What they intended to do was to shame and humiliate the girls. Even if the physician reported virgin status for any girl, Mrs. Beatty said that as punishment for being AWOL, it was appropriate that the girl had been forced to undergo the humiliation of a pelvic exam, performed not for medical reasons but as punishment. She was quite sure that her sense of justice was reasonable, and that this type of humili -

41

ation was a fair and appropriate punishment.

When confronted with the argument that no such humiliation was imposed on the boys who went AWOL, the Beatty's said, "That's just the way it is."

Later, they barred this window of the girls' dorm. The "bars" was actually a metal gate, I guess so that it wouldn't look like so bad, wouldn't look like prison bars to the outside world.

***

Every year a group went "tagging" in downtown Chicago to raise money for the Children's Home. This group of "taggers" included Home staffers, Free Methodist Church members, and the older, more mature kids. We caravanned into the city, the kids in the two VW Microbuses, and the adults in several cars.

How my heart sunk when I was let out on my corner, and I stood watching the Microbus sputter away. The other kids and adults would be likewise dropped at their tagging corners, "somewhere nearby," I was assured, but out of my view.

I could hardly force myself to approach a stranger and ask him to deposit money into my tin can. But soon I got up the courage to stop a passer-by. I looked up at the suited businessman, carrying the Chicago *Tribune* under his arm, square in the face, held up my red tin can and asked, "Would you like to contribute to the Woodstock Children's Home?"

He carefully deposited what seemed to be all his pocket change into the narrow slot on top of the can. The coins clinked gleefully as they fell in, hitting the bottom of my empty can. I was so pleased. I thanked him and gave him a red, triangular tag with a string attached to it. On the bus ride into the city, we'd been given the job of tying a knot around the two ends of the short strings of all the tags in our box, so that they could be affixed to a button. My business-man donor wrapped the string several times around his jacket button and then patted the red triangle tag with a flourish. "There," he said smiling at me, and he strode away purposefully, proudly displaying his red tag which read, "I contributed to the Woodstock Children's Home."

***

The Home was incorporated as the Chicago Industrial Home for Children, in September 1888; it was founded in Chicago by the Rev. T. B. Arnold, a Free Methodist minister. It was moved to Woodstock on March 19, 1891 after a Woodstock resident, Mrs. Roxey D. Stevens donated her farm as a home for the orphaned children. In 1967, sixty children lived at the Home.

In October 1966, the 5½-acre Fox Farm on Kishwaukee Valley Road was purchased for $70,000.00 and remodeled to use as a Group Home; it housed seven boys and nine girls from six families. I went to work there as soon as it opened, as an "Assistant Child Care Worker." I was sixteen years old and going into my senior year of high school. I drove out every afternoon after school in my VW and worked until 9:00 p.m., and also on Saturdays.

Then, pursuing the group home plans, on Seminary Avenue close to the Main Building, the Spruce, Pine, and Cedar cottages were opened in 1971-72 to house teenagers.

However, after this level of real estate expansion and forward planning, the Home, which had opera-ted continuously since its incorporation in 1888, abruptly ceased operations and was entirely closed three years later.

Reasons reported were: "changing philosophies regarding child welfare services . . . the increasing encroachment of the state Department of Children and Family Services . . . and the continual increase in the cost."

The Rev. Clifford Redding, executive director of the Woodstock Children's Home and Sunset Manor since 1959, said at that time, "A change in policy by the Illinois DCFS, beginning with the administration of former Gov. Dan Walker, made the board's decision inevitable."

Redding further explained that "One of the original intents for the facility, which never actually was realized, was to train children to prepare them with skills for entry into the job market." I certainly agree with him about that failure.

My sister and I, as well as many other kids, had been placed in the Home by, and were under the legal guardianship of, the Evangelical Child Welfare Agency, of Chicago. One of their social workers was the red-head who had driven us to the Home in her Volkswagen bug back in 1963. Throughout the years, we were aware of the ECWA's presence and connection to the Home but had infrequent contact with Agency representatives.

Just before high school graduation, I contacted Ms. Wheeling, then executive director of the ECWA, and asked for an appointment with her. I rode the train into Chicago and visited her at the ECWA's 127 North Dearborn Street fifth-floor office. I told her of my concerns about the Home: about the solitary confinement room, about Bud's tragedy, about the virginity tests, about how Mr. Beatty was always ogling Carol's body; and the lewd comments he made in her presence. Carol was one of the girls who, as Mrs.

44

Beatty had informed us all, flunked the virginity tests. I named names and registered every complaint I could think of that had troubled me.

I expected nothing to come of my conversation with Ms. Wheeling. The ECWA hadn't been very visible over the years, letting us just idle along. Why should they become interested in me or my concerns when they were soon to be rid of me?

To my surprise, Ms. Wheeling, a morbidly obese, never-married woman with lots of latent male energy, seemed to be sincerely interested in what I said, and seemed to take my comments seriously. She told me that she'd look into my complaints; even so, I believed that would be the last I'd hear from her.

Awhile later I contacted her and again I was surprised at what she said. She told me that the ECWA had fully investigated my complaints along with "some other things," including a "scandal" involving my sister. She said that I "might be interested in knowing" that as result of their findings, they were never again going to place any more children in the Woodstock Children's Home. And after the kids they'd already placed there had graduated, that would be the end of their association with the Home. My sister, who was one year behind me in school, was the youngest of the ECWA's wards. She graduated in 1971, and the Home closed soon thereafter.

The ECWA was the Home's largest "customer," for placement of children, so the withdrawal of this business was a huge loss, not to mention the public relations ramifications.

At the time, I was surprised at this outcome; I hadn't really expected anything to come of my complaints, but what I told Ms. Wheeling may have surely gotten her attention.

It is also possible that the ECWA was not going to place any more children at the Woodstock Children's

Home, or anywhere, for that matter. It's possible that Ms. Wheeling knew at the time I met with her of the imminent demise of the ECWA also. The Evangelical Child & Family Agency did also eventually close.

Because we'd been neglected and abused all our lives, we kids weren't always able to discern improper, inappropriate, abusive or illegal treatment of us. And even if we were able to ascertain it, we often did not have the self-confidence to speak up for ourselves against our abusers.

It seems that my complaints to Ms. Wheeling may have been at least one factor in why the Home closed so abruptly. I have never known where those approximately sixty kids went when the Home closed.

5. A Burden on Society

*"...has been a junior staff member and con-
tributed to the Home...will be welcomed back as one
who has achieved..."*

*from my 1970 Woodstock Children's Home
"Discharge Summary"*

Once I wrote a letter and hand delivered it to the executive director of the Home, asking for some new underwear. I had previously asked the house parents for the underwear, but they told me that a requisition for such a princely sum of money must be obtained from the executive director, and they were not willing to ask for it on my behalf.

I wrote this letter in great indignation on July 9, 1965, the day of my thirteenth birthday, because on that day, I was grounded by the house parents as punishment for being late to the breakfast table. The reason I was late, as I explained in the letter, was because I had no underwear. I was outraged at being treated so childishly and unjustly.

In the letter, I referred to his air-conditioned office, implying that if the Home could afford his nicely appointed, air-conditioned office, then certainly the Home could spare a couple of dollars to purchase some underwear for me. In those days, air-conditioning was uncommon; his was the only room or office at the Home which was air conditioned.

My letter was polite and well written but with just an edge of outrage; and I seriously needed some new underwear. Nevertheless, Mr. Redding apparently considered my letter impudent, and it sorely burned him. The next day after school, my house parent told me that Mr. Redding, the executive director of the Woodstock Children's Home and the Sunset Manor, wanted to see me in his office.

Mr. Redding was tall, fine boned, and slender; he moved gracefully and aristocratically. He spoke softly and never deviated from his mild demeanor. He was aloof, reserved, and somewhat saturnine. We kids never observed any display of warmth or pleasure from him, toward anyone, or about anything. I never saw him smile; he maintained a disapproving affect in all his interactions, even with the house parents.

He was bald and had a prominent nose. His eyes were close set and he had a small mouth full of crooked teeth. This gave him a profile of the American Bald Eagle. We kids joked constantly about his appearance and about his reserved nature. We called him Baldy or the Bald Eagle; it was a perfect likeness. We said that he was so skinny that he had to run around in the shower to get wet. We said that his head was a mosquito landing patch. We speculated endlessly and with great imagination as to how he and his wife, who was even more aloof and aristocratic than he, could have possibly deigned to copulate in order to conceive their two children.

I walked to his office and timidly knocked on the door. The door was always shut, probably to keep the air conditioning in. He told me to come in, shut the door behind me, and sit down. I sank lowly into a large chair in front of his desk. The air conditioner hummed quietly from the window. Through the top pane of the window, I could see some of the kids, having obediently arrived home from school on time, their clothes hurriedly changed, already outside playing on the merry-go-round.

He spoke slowly and deliberately, quietly but

48

sternly. His neck and cheeks were flushed. He told me with great constraint and understatement that he didn't appreciate my letter.

He told me that my father had never paid one dime for my support at the Home; and I certainly did not doubt him on that.

He told me that I was a burden on society and that I "was here" only because of the benevolence of the Free Methodist Church.

He told me that I should be grateful for all I had, and that I should never ask for anything ever again. Then rising slowly from his chair, he glared down at me and, nodding toward the closed door, he dismissed me.

***

Rule Book

We were given a rule book which made a huge effort to be comprehensive and to micromanage every imaginable issue and behavior. I still have my original copy of the *Rule Book,* in which seventy-seven different subjects are covered by one or more rules. Subjects included are: academic probation, church attendance, proper dress and personal grooming, employment, haircuts, mail, permissions and privileges, radios and record players, visitation with family and friends, television, study halls and seating arrangements at the dining room table and at the Free Methodist church.

Prohibited activities included dancing or going to school dances, playing cards, going to theatres, smoking and drinking alcohol (both illegal). The thirty-six-page Rule Book included such rules of decorum and etiquette as:

"When you enter the dining room, you are to do so without conversation. You will stand behind your chair until after the prayer has been offered," and

"Bread shall be broken in half before being buttered."

A couple of rules that charm me most are: "Transportation to and/or from school will be provided (but you will not be required to ride) in the event of temperatures below 10 degrees above zero."

And: "Each child fifteen years of age or in high school not earning an average of $3.00 per week from employment will be given $2.00 per week for personal spending. Those receiving an allowance of $2.00 per week will be expected to purchase their own personal needs such as cosmetics and toilet items. In addition, they will purchase their school supplies as needed . . ."

Another rule is: "Incoming mail will be delivered daily to your house parent. The Home reserves the right to open any of your mail which they feel may be injurious to you. It is not our intent to withhold any mail from you. In fact, we encourage regular correspondence with your family and friends as long as it is positive, wholesome, and realistic. If you receive a letter which your caseworker feels should not be delivered to you, you will be informed and told the reason."

The *Rule Book* includes a daily schedule which accounts for every hour of our day from 6:30 a.m. to 10:00 p.m. for seven days a week.

Another rule states: "Only rarely is it possible for a teenager to own or operate a motorized vehicle of any kind. Any approval for such must come from the Executive Director of the Home."

I was able and was allowed to buy a 1965 Volkswagen convertible bug when I was sixteen years old. I paid for it with approximately $500.00 of my own money that I'd earned working, mostly at the Sunset Manor, and a loan from the Home State Bank in Woodstock for $500.00. The social worker Ira McIntyre held the title; he co-signed my bank loan and included me on his personal Country Companies Insurance (a division of Farm Mutual) policy. But I made the $52.00 per six months payment directly to the insurance company and the monthly car payment directly to the bank.

Mr. McIntyre made it very clear to me that if I defaulted on the bank loan, the insurance payments, or the maintenance, he'd take over ownership of the car. When I was eighteen, the car was re-titled in my name. My pride in ownership of that car, my strong motivation to keep the car, and the personal and economic freedom it provided me were certainly what kept me out of trouble and enabled me to endure my teenage years.

I can't imagine to this day why I was allowed to buy the car or how I was able to pay for the car as I did. But I did pay for every cent of that car, including the insurance and maintenance. Certainly the reason I was allowed to buy this car was to provide myself transportation to and from my job at the Kishwaukee Valley cottage, the group home on the outskirts of town owned by the Woodstock Children's Home where I was employed as an "Assistant Childcare Worker."

I had started working for the Homes at the Sunset Manor, a skilled nursing care and rest home facility, a few months before my fifteenth birthday. Then the summer before my senior year in high school, Mr. Redding asked me to work, as an assistant child care worker, at the new Kishwaukee Valley Cottage which was on the southwestern outskirts of town about eight miles away.

Over spring vacation in my senior year, I was allowed to drive my Volkswagen alone to Tennessee to visit two universities there which were of interest to me, and also to visit my two younger brothers, who lived in a Children's Home there. I marvel to this day that I was allowed to make this long trip, driving my car alone, much less that they allowed me to drive my own car. I was the only kid I know of in the Home allowed to purchase a car (remember, I was a girl at the time), although Willie, a boy several years older than I, was allowed to buy a motorcycle.

On the return trip home from Tennessee I got into some bad weather; the fog was so thick I couldn't see more than a few feet in front of me, causing me to drive no more than thirty-five miles an hour, all the way up Route 47. Consequently, I arrived in Woodstock much later than planned, at about 2:00 a.m. The Kishwaukee Valley Cottage was locked and I didn't have a key.

I couldn't awaken anyone to come downstairs and open the door, as all bedrooms were upstairs. So, I drove into Woodstock and across town to house parent Mr. Leed's house. I was afraid that after driving all the way to Tennessee and back with no mishaps, I'd get picked up by the local police for violating the curfew laws, as I was only seventeen.

I arrived at the Leeds house, he let me in, and I slept in his recliner chair in their living room until daylight sneaked through the windows and across the carpet. He was cheerful first thing in the morning, and a big coffee drinker; he made coffee for us in an aluminum pot that he boiled on the stove. When it started to percolate he watched the color of the coffee in the transparent knob on the lid and whisked it from the flame before it got too dark. He poured the aromatic, stoutly blended coffee into two large mugs; we drank it black. Then he sat down holding his large steaming mug in both hands and with the cordiality that one adult would extend to another during a coffee klatch, he fixed his total attention on me and asked, "So how did your trip go? Tell me all about it."

***

"I have a dream..."
Martin Luther King, March 1963

For my high school graduation in June 1970, I received a blue Samsonite suitcase from the Home, which I still have. They invited to move out of the staff quarters, where I'd stayed since shortly after beginning work at the Kishwaukee Valley Cottage in my senior year. Everything I owned fit into my convertible VW. Coincidently I both left the Home and had arrived at the home as a kid, in a Volkswagen bug.

What tumultuous and bewildering decade the sixties, when I was growing up in the Children's Home. On February 20, 1962, John Herschel Glenn, who was born in July, in Cambridge, Ohio, both month and town same as me, completed the first manned spacecraft orbital mission, in the Mercury-Atlas *Friendship 7*.

The Cuban Missile Crisis in October 1962 had been narrowly averted just several months before Esther and I were sent to the Home, on March 28, 1963.

Later that year, John F. Kennedy was assassinated on November 22, 1963. I, like many other Americans, remember exactly where I was, at the time. I was sitting in the second row, third seat in my sixth grade class at Olson Junior High School, in Woodstock, Illinois, when the school principal gravely announced over the scratchy-sounding loudspeaker, "Attention, attention, President Kennedy has been shot."

That night, we Home kids and house parents gathered around the twelve-inch, black and white television with a "rabbit-ears" antenna; and dumbfounded, we watched the countless reruns of the live account of that presidential motor procession through the streets of Dallas, lined with crowds of onlookers; and then the shocking crack of that fatal shot.

On July 2, 1964, the Civil Rights Act was enacted, banning racial discrimination in all public places, outlawing racial discrimination by employers and unions, and withdrawing federal funds from state programs that discriminated against black people.

On April 4, 1968, Martin Luther King was assassinated, and soon later, on June 6, 1968, Robert F. Kennedy was assassinated. My thanks to Dion for his memorial tune, "Abraham, Martin and John," which was number four on the pop charts later that year." I still get choked up when I hear it today.

With the decade's backdrop of the Vietnam War increasingly pounding the conscience of Americans, the anxiety of the draft, the My Lai atrocity, the illegal and brutal bombing of Cambodia; I heard drumbeats of great concern. The turmoil of American society was growing to dangerous proportions.

Simmering under the overt social turmoil was our "Russian paranoia," which was made manifest by regular air-raid drills in school, and the construction of bomb fall-out shelters in the city. This paranoia had seized Americans in 1957 with the advent of the Soviet's orbiting satellite *Sputnik I*. And then four years later, the Soviet Union launched the first manned satellite. Americans were shocked and spooked; and scrambling to gain the lead in a fierce competition with the Soviet Union's space program, the National Aeronautics and Space Administration (NASA) was hastily created in 1958.

The Chicago Police Riot, at the Democratic National Convention, in August 1968, was battled out on Michigan Avenue near Grant Park and Roosevelt University, where for several days Chicago police clashed with thousands of civil rights and anti-Vietnam War protesters.

Amid the nightmare of events which followed Martin Luther King's soaring dream speech in 1963, was the surrealistic event on July 20, 1969, of Apollo 11 astronauts' Neil Armstrong and Edwin "Buzz" Aldrin's walk on the moon.

Then on May 4, 1970, one month before my high school graduation, National Guardsmen fired into a crowd of protesters at Kent State University, in Ohio, killing four students and wounding nine others.

What a tumultuous and bewildering decade indeed! What a frightening world to be shoved out into, when I was discharged from the Children's Home in June 1970, just as the Beatles were singing "Let It Be," the number one hit in 1970.

I moved out of the Children's Home facilities immediately, as I was invited to do; and I did not attend my graduation ceremony or any of the many graduation parties and celebrations.

After I left the Children's Home, I never received any communications from them, not a letter or phone call. They never once mailed me the Home's newsletter, *The Woodstock Friend.* I was neither contacted by the Children's Home nor the Agency which had placed me there.

Part Three

Parents
(1929 & 1931 to 1965)

6. Mother

If you look at a U.S. map, because of its shape and location, Ohio looks like the heart of our great nation. Its main artery then is The National Road, old U.S. Route 40, which runs east and west across the entire state, through Cambridge, Zanesville, and Columbus. The National Road was the first highway built with federal funds; it was authorized by Congress in 1806 during the Jefferson administration. Beginning in Cumberland, Maryland, it runs 600 miles and terminates in Vandalia, Illinois.

Zanesville is home of the famous "Y" Bridge, originally built in 1814 as part of the National Road. It crossing the confluence of the Muskingum and Licking Rivers. "It is the only bridge in the world you can cross and still be on the same side of the river."

"S" bridges, referring to the bridges' approach to, and span of the creek, are also part of the National Road, in this area.

If you travel south from Zanesville on Route 60 in the springtime, keeping the Muskingum River on your right, you can smell the honeysuckle most all the way down. The highway follows the meandering river and after a short drive into Duncan Falls, you come to a bridge on your right. Crossing over the Muskingum River here brings you into the tiny town of Philo, where my mother was born.

Between 1910 and 1920, a baseball team was called the "Zanesville Flood Sufferers," and you can imagine how they came up with that name.

My mother was born on February 13, 1931, at home in Philo, the ninth of ten children to Hilda Louise Fisher, a German Roman Catholic, and Ora Hampton Harrop, an Anglican. "What a combination," she used to say sarcastically.

She always told the story that they'd named her Joy because she was born after five boys. What a beautiful name, but sadly and ironically I can't remember anything joyous about her.

My mother's home was a two-hundred-sixty-acre farm, on Back Run Road, in the rural, rolling hills of southeastern Ohio. Her mother, Hilda Louise, was born in a house nearby, on the same road, which still stands.

Three old country school buildings, no longer in use, also stand on Back Run Road. Before he was the twentieth President of the United States, James A. Garfield taught in one of those schools. The old school bell, from the school in which Garfield taught, is now in the front of the Harrop homestead.

My maternal grandfather Ora's ancestors were pioneer settlers in Muskingum County and have been in the area since 1826, when Joy's great-grandfather Aquilla Harrop traveled by wagon to Brush Creek Township in Muskingum County, from Loudoun County, Virginia, at age twelve, with his parents James and Mary (Cohogan) Harrop.

James Harrop's father was born in England, a soldier in the English army and a weaver by trade. Upon arrival in Muskingum County, James bought 160 acres of unimproved land and began to clear it.

Aquilla Harrop, was a life-long Republican and Methodist; he and his wife Sarah French had eleven children including Stephen, who was my mother's grandfather.

Stephen and his two brothers, Grafton and Jacob, fought in the Civil War. In 1861, Grafton and Jacob both enlisted in the Sixty-Second Ohio Regiment Company A. Grafton died in the night charge, made famous by the movie *Glory,* on Fort Wagner at Charleston, South Carolina. He was killed instantly while advancing with his regiment on July 18, 1863. Grafton was buried on the field on which he fought and died.

Jacob received a severe wound in the thigh in the same battle, and he lay on the field until the following day, when he fell into the hands of the rebels. He was sent back to the Union lines and entered the hospital near New York City, where he died on August 1, 1863.

Stephen enlisted in Company F, 178th Ohio Volunteer Infantry and served in Schofield's army corps.

John, another son of Aquilla, was a prominent and successful teacher in Muskingum county schools.

In addition to those three of Aquilla's sons in the Union army, he also had two brothers who fought for the Union, Stephen in an Ohio regiment and William in an Illinois regiment.

The Harrop homestead in Philo was inherited by my mother's brother, Robert, the seventh son, upon the death of their father, Ora.

Her family "didn't do much farming," as she told me, but instead they had seven oil wells and three gas wells on their property, which they contracted out to government and utilities mining companies.

I remember a charming photograph of my mother as a teenager, in a red and white gingham dress with a V-neckline and a cinched waist, posing coyly inside the base of one of the oil derricks on their property. My mother spoke often, and with much pride and yearning, about her home in southeastern Ohio. I remember her saying countless times, during the time I knew her, "I want to go home, I want to go home."

My mother lived a very sheltered and pampered

life. Her father doted on his five daughters, but was very stern with his sons, she told me. My mother seemed to be awed by her father and respected him very much.

When she was old enough to attend high school, her father bought a home in McConnelsville, a small, historic town farther south along the Muskingum River in the area through which the "longest raid of the civil war" rampaged, Morgan's Raid, a terrorizing guerrilla force of 2,500 Confederate cavalrymen.

She proudly graduated from Malta & McConnelsville High School and always wore on her left hand her gold high school class ring, which said, "M & M High School, Class of 1949."

Her father bought the other home in town so that she would not have to ride the school bus from their farm in Philo to McConnelsville, nowadays an approximately thirty-minute drive south of Philo on the scenic state Route 60. While school was in season, she and her sister Patty and their mother stayed at their town home in McConnelsville during the week.

***

Poem Within A Poem

I wrote the following poem at age
fourteen while living in the
Children's Home after finding
my mother languishing in
the Elgin State Mental Hospital.
Reading it after so many years is
like finding my old baby pictures:
staring and studying, I recognize myself.

61

Perhaps it's finally the eyes in the baby
photo through which I see myself, and
after some embarrassment I do accept,
yes, that is a photograph of me.
Rereading this poem thirty years later,
I feel compassion for myself as a youth
and I realize that at the time, I
couldn't let it be known just how
innocent I was not. My poem expresses
anger and cynicism, also an effort
idealism. There is, I cringe to
say it, some missionary zeal
but no messianic complex, so
common in sensitive youths. As
I recognize my eyes in the baby picture,
I recognize that the soul of this poem is me.
And at any age and in any form
I can now recognize myself and accept myself,
though this may cause some uneasiness.

Commitment

One sunny breezy day
I took it upon myself
to look upon the faces
of those who are
rejected, forgotten.
It was easy to recognize
that look of defeat
no smiles
no frowns
not a trace of emotion
anywhere
in the faces of those
who know of no
Hope
in the future.

I wondered where
will it all end,
at death's inevitable visit?
I was once told of the love
and justice and mercy of God;
I have already learned about people
but God must not know of this place.

One sunny breezy day
under the shade of my own apathy
I cried; and when there were
no more tears, I was filled with hate
toward all the other forests of apathy
And I vowed to do something.

I could not write this
then but I can now.
After I found out where she was,
I convinced an older friend
to borrow Mr. Leed's car,
a Rambler with a three-speed
transmission under the steering wheel.
We drove to the administration building
where I beseeched a matronly lady
who peered at me from behind
a foot-square window with metal bars.
After suffering my request,
she with great caution, slid open
the window, said a few words,
then slammed it shut again.
My heart was pounding, she
seemed to be checking a roster;
then she spat out
the name of the building
through the cracked window
and slammed it shut again.
I didn't dare ask for directions

I went to several buildings
before I found the right one.
I rang a bell at the door
which was jarring even
to my outside ears;
it made a bellowing blast
several times before
another woman came and peered
at me through another
small window just above my head.
She yelled out, "What do you want?"
"I want to see my mother,"
"And who is she?"
I hated yelling at a thick door
but shouted back again
"Her name is Joy Hall,"
thinking again what a cruel
paradox her name, Joy.
The huge door groaned open and
immediately I was taken by the
stench of an uncomfortably warm,
large, open room. The windows were
locked, barred, and nailed shut.
One fan buzzed in the hazy blue,
hypnotically hot, stenchfully stuffy,
cigarette-smoke-filled room.
Here the residents were languishing;
some of them eyed me curiously,
most of them were dozing. Two
approached me aggressively. I looked
for a clue from the attendant,
she signaled that the aggressors
were harmless though annoying,
and that I needn't be concerned.
Still I was uneasy.
The woman told me to "Stay"
and walked away leaving

me standing in the middle
of the dark room.
Many of the residents
were coming and going,
moving about with no purpose.
After some time a woman
approached me from out of nowhere.
She was fat and utterly unkempt,
puffing maniacally on a cigarette,
laughing obnoxiously,
inappropriately. I was
uneasy as she persisted.
After all these years,
I still can't find the words
to describe how I felt
when she called out
my name.
I knew I was there
to find my mother
after so many years
in a state mental institution,
but no amount of preparation
could have spared me from
the emotional slaying.
I couldn't breathe; for a moment
it seemed my legs would collapse
under me. I struggled to maintain
my balance and composure.
I hadn't recognized my mother
and furthermore, I was shocked
and offended at the sight of her.
Her face was filthy;
her clothes were torn and
falling off her. Her fingers
were stained with tobacco and
she stank same as the rest of the place.
As I stood facing her

the residents eyed me scornfully.
I was slipping and sliding, spinning
on emotional ice. I willed myself
to keep from falling to my feelings.
I had remembered my mother as pretty,
with green eyes and chestnut-colored hair;
well-groomed, her hands always clean,
smelling like bleach, instead of
tobacco stained and stinking.
She'd always been quiet and shy.
I remembered she'd sing softly
to herself and sometimes make
a soft sucking sound between her teeth,
reassuring to me as a child.
Though I have no recollection
of her holding me in her arms
or even holding my hand,
I knew she'd never in
a million years smoke a cigarette.
I'd never heard her laugh out loud,
she'd always acted feminine
and demure. Somehow I managed
to get through several minutes of a visit;
conversation was unbearably
forced and superficial. She
seemed unaffected by seeing me,
unaware and casual.
I was ashamed
when I ended the visit
after a few awkward moments
but I couldn't have stood
it any longer. Yet Joy hadn't
seemed to care if I stayed or left,
whether I was there or not.
She didn't ask me to return and
this was sad and confusing for me.
I was never so happy to walk

out into the fresh air;
there sat Willie in the Rambler
waiting patiently for me. God!
was I glad to see him. The best
friend I ever had. He was his usual
upbeat, outgoing and affable self.
I opened the door, hopped in and said,
"Let's get the hell out of here."
Good friend that he was, he sensed
my misery and tried to engage me
in distracting conversation, but
I couldn't say much all the way home.
So you see, I couldn't have told it
like this when I wrote "Commitment."
I was living in a Children's Home
then, unable to help myself
much less her.

7. Father

Prima Gravida

In the photo they're standing side by side,
confident stances, shining smiles,
husband and wife. His name is Forest;
hers is Esther, after the beautiful Biblical
Jewish princess who saved her people.
They're dressed in their best;
he in a three-piece, chalk-striped suit,
white tie, white shirt with curved collar,
white broad-banded Panama hat.
He stands tall, shoulders proud, feet firm
in black leather serious shoes.
Tortoise-shell glasses; a fountain pen
in his lapel pocket. Look closely;
you can see that he wears a gold
Christian cross on a gold chain.
The cross is drawn up and fastened
to the center button of his vest.
He'd been a minister for
fifty years when he retired. During the same
time he was thrice elected Republican
Representative to the Ohio State Legislature.
The Reverend Honorable
Forest Webster Hall, graduate of Ohio
Wesleyan University, Muskingum College,
and Moody Bible Institute, Chicago,
the West Point of Christian service,
as a pennant on one of his old notebooks
declares. His left arm encircles his wife;
she had been beloved of him
since her earliest years:
in the photo she is twenty-two
and he is thirty-eight. He had

watched her and waited for her
to grow into womanhood. I know this
and other secret desires of her heart;
I have three of her diaries
wherein she recorded
her innocent yearnings of him
while they were dating.
They were the darling lovers
of their day; highly favored,
they did everything right and
could do no wrong; their
families blessed their courtship.
She in a blousy, taffeta spring coat,
long silk neck scarf, a cloche hat,
and open toed shoes. Her piano-virtuoso
hands are clasped delicately
at the length of her relaxed arms.
Look closely now; can you see that
she is gently pregnant? Six months.
Six months *prima gravida*.
She died just two months
after smiling for this photo;
she died giving birth
to my father. Esther was
Forest's precious flower
and she died in thrashing
convulsions, a most
hideous and violent death
and she never saw her baby.

***

Within the first few minutes of meeting my father, Paul, he'd find a way to slip into the conversation the fact that his mother died while giving birth to him; he did this all his life. My brother Phillip, ten years younger than I and reared apart from my sister and me, by my father and his second wife, confirms that this is also what Paul did when he was growing up. Paul was a gifted con man, and he was always trying to get others' sympathy, always implying some excuse for the mess he had made of his life and the mess he made of my and my sister's childhoods.

He was also violent with my two younger brothers, his step-children, and their pet dogs when they were all growing up in east Tennessee. The violence got so disruptive that my brothers went to live with one of their high school teachers through graduation. His step-children hated him and wouldn't have anything to do with him. After their mother died, they ran him out of their childhood home.

During her pregnancy, my father's mother developed eclampsia, then kidney failure, and died of uremic poisoning giving birth to him by Caesarean section, on June 23, 1929. Her tragic death occurred before the technology of kidney dialysis. She was just twenty-one years old and in her first pregnancy. Thanks to my brother Phillip, I have in my possession three of her personal diaries, which she kept before her marriage to my grandfather. They reveal her charm, innocence, inner beauty and her love and devotion to her husband Forest. They are the most precious books I have.

I'd always heard her described as a "genius," excelling in music; I was told she studied at the university at age sixteen. I realize that her death must have devastated my grandfather. He had known her family and had waited patiently for her to grow up, so he could marry her. Fortunately, she was never in disagreement with his plan. She was twenty; he was thirty-five and never previously married on their wedding day in April 1927.

I have a handwritten letter of my grandfather's written in 1964, one year before his death. In it he lovingly told of her and their pastoral and evangelistic work together; he described his wife Esther as a "girl evangelist, an efficient soul winner," saying "She was quite a musician." She ministered in the jail, prisons, and work houses in Columbus, and the girls' reformatory at Marysville, according to his letter. She was the daughter of George Washington Robey, a United Brethren minister, who died when Esther was thirteen.

My father had epilepsy and suffered *grand mal* seizures, which started when he was about two years old and were believed to have been caused by birth anoxia and his mother's death of eclampsia and uremia during delivery.

He was cared for and doted on by his father's three sisters and also by his deceased mother's mother, who lived to be elderly; I even remember her. There was no shortage in my grandfather's large family, church family, and among his political colleagues, of persons available and eager to help raise my father. I remember very well my grandfather's three sisters and three brothers. I remember observing their interactions on several occasions, at family reunions and gatherings; and I saw them to be unconditionally loving and supportive of my father and of us, his family. I was happier around my grandfather and his family than around anyone else, especially my parents.

My father enrolled at Muskingum College in New Concord, proud *alma mater* of astronaut and Ohio Senator, John Glenn. I remember a formal college photograph taken of the basketball team which included Paul as a guard. "He finished two years of college," as his father used to brag. My mother said he flunked out after two years. I remember him angrily claiming that it was because he had to "bum rides" to school, from home in neighboring Cambridge. I'm sure he was angry and humiliated at his inability to drive himself, but I doubt he had to "bum rides," given his pampered upbringing within an extended family of abundant resources; a family which spoiled him, most certainly because of the tragic circumstances of his mother's death and his subsequent epilepsy.

My father could never get a driver's license, of course. Today a young man could hardly conduct his life if he couldn't drive. I never saw my father behind the wheel of a car; and he could never have afforded a car anyway.

I have the original court order that my grandfather obtained in 1949, naming him the legal guardian of my father when he was seventeen years old. This can only mean that my grandfather didn't think my father fully capable of managing his own affairs; and as my father approached legal maturity, his father grew concerned. This obtaining legal guardianship was a responsible act by my grandfather, but I'm sure it enraged my father. I frequently heard him proclaim, "Dad is not going to run my life."

My grandfather could have been happy to get rid of the spoiled brat, who failed at everything he ever attempted, who raged at him constantly, and who reminded him daily that he lost his most beloved wife in order to have such a good-for-nothing, epileptic, and angry son. But instead he bragged about his son, telling everyone that Paul preached his first sermon, entitled "The Three Trees," at age nine. He bragged about my father being able to play the piano by ear, easily transposing from one key to another, that he could pick up any musical instrument and play it without instruction, including the piano, a coronet, trumpet, bass tuba, autoharp, guitar, and mandolin—he could even play a saw— and that he had a ministerial appointment in the Ohio Methodist Conference before going to Moody Bible Institute, in Chicago.

My grandfather was always kind and loving; and I never heard him raise his voice in protest to my father's angry tirades against him. My grandfather was intelligent, long-suffering, generous, successful, and charismatic; and I'm sure that my father hoped to get out of his father's shadow by moving to Chicago, as he later did.

Unfortunately the guiding force in my father's life seemed to be revenge against his father. And he was quite willing to sabotage his marriage and our childhood to cause his father pain. I'd heard several of his family and my mother wondering out loud, even asking my father directly, whatever could it be that caused him to hate his father so much? I never heard of another person who disliked my grandfather. Whenever I was with him, at family reunions, the fair grounds, or at church, we were surrounded by friendly people, which caused my grandfather to beam with enjoyment.

My mother told me that they had married against both their parents' strongest objections, especially her parents'. They knew of his epilepsy and forbade her to marry him. In those days, epilepsy was talked about in whispers.

My grandfather died just two years after we were placed in the Children's Home. Both he and his sister Grace had consistently offered to take Esther and me into their homes; I have copies of handwritten letters by both of them to this effect. My father never told his father and aunt that he'd given us away; that he'd given up our guardianship and made us wards of the State of Illinois. When they finally found out about it, my grandfather was mortally heartbroken.

My grandfather begged him to "Come home," where relatives on both sides could be supportive. He offered to give my father a house in Cambridge for us to live in. My mother, my sister Esther, and I could not have been happier with the idea, but my father stubbornly refused. When my grandfather Forest died in August 1965, I asked my mother what was the cause of his death, and she told me that "he died of a broken heart."

Part Four

Early Childhood in Chicago
(1952-1963)

8. North Pine Grove

Hope is the thing with feathers,
That perches in the soul
And sings the tune without the words,
And never stops at all.

Emily Dickinson

I was six months old and my mother was pregnant with my sister when we moved from Cambridge, Ohio, to Chicago in January 1953. After flunking out of Muskingum College, my father came to Chicago for the opportunity of attending Moody Bible Institute with his father's financial support, and at the same time to get out from under his shadow. Paul knew he could never live up to his father's reputation.

My grandfather had graduated from Moody in the riot-torn Chicago, of 1919. In this year race riots broke out in twenty-five Northern cities, the bloodiest racial strife since the Civil War. The rioting was ugliest in Chicago with thirty-eight dead, 537 injured, and whole Chicago neighborhoods were burned and looted.

Paul also wanted to avoid being accountable to his local Methodist Bishop. He was already an ordained Methodist minister when we left for Chicago. His ordination was certainly facilitated by his father, who had served as a Methodist minister fifty years by the time of his retirement.

Before my father left for Chicago, he'd had a falling out with his Methodist Bishop and likely his decision to move to Chicago and attend Moody Bible Institute was also his scheme to avoid official reprimand by his Bishop.

Over the course of his life, whenever my father has fouled up, Paul's way of dealing with conflict has been to move far away. It has been his lifelong pattern to deny any and all of his mistakes, to run away from all accountability, and to stubbornly believe in the doctrine of "the eternal salvation of the believer." As long as he believed that "Jesus died for my sins," he "was saved," period, end of it. As a result of his believing this, he thought he needn't ever have to deal with the consequences of his behavior, or otherwise be held accountable, or responsible to anyone for his sins. "It's between only me and God," he'd say. "I'm under the blood of Jesus."

We first settled at 3624 North Pine Grove Avenue, in a north side Jewish neighborhood along Lake Michigan. We occupied two tiny, adjacent "English basement" apartments in a large, blond brick apartment building. Esther and I slept in the two-room front apartment, and my parents stayed in the back apartment.

I remember it was possible to hear the crowds roaring at Wrigley Field on a summer afternoon after the Cubs scored a home run. I have pleasant memories of living there but I was acutely aware that my mother was terrified of living in Chicago, and my father was hypervigilant. Both of them went to great lengths to imbue me with their fears and anxieties, telling me in detail every news account of murder and rape. I recall my mother was greatly upset when the Anshe Emet Synagogue, still at 3760 North Pine Grove, was bombed.

When I was two-and-a-half years old, my mother's father died, whereupon she suffered the first of many "nervous breakdowns." At this time in 1955, Esther and I were first made dependent wards of the state and placed in foster care, with a family named the

DeGroots. Over the years, before we finally ended up in the Woodstock Children's Home, we were shuttled back and forth to various temporary homes, including church families' homes and relatives' homes from both sides of the family in Ohio, "for a visit."

Esther was miserable at the DeGroots and the other temporary homes, although she seemed miserable all the time, wherever she was. It seemed to me that all she did was cry and throw temper tantrums, and I saw that she always got away with this. I noticed that my father was remarkably restrained when she bawled and carried on.

But I didn't dare cry much less throw a temper tantrum. I learned very young that one peep out of me would instantly result in my father's fist smashing my face, and so I was relieved to be anywhere away from my parents.

And during Esther's frequent crying and public temper tantrums, I was annoyed and embarrassed for her, and thought, *Geez Esther would you shut up and get a hold of yourself!*

Additionally, I went to church camp each summer. I sensed my parents were always trying to get rid of me, and that was why they allowed me to spend as much time as possible at church summer camp.

I don't recall Esther ever going to camp with me. I doubt she could have tolerated being separated from her mother, and in a strange place for that length of time. But I was always happy for a chance to be out of the house and away from my parents, mostly my father. I was terrified of him from my earliest memory.

These various temporary outplacements always coincided with some "family crisis" and my mother's recurring institutionalizations. Each time we were eventually returned to our parents, until March 1963, when we were placed in the Children's Home.

I've always wondered why my parents didn't

return to their families in southeastern Ohio after my father flunked out of Moody Bible Institute in the first year, or at any time thereafter. But now I know that my father was just too stubborn and my mother was too ashamed to return home.

I remember seeing my mother's father alive. I later recounted this event to my mother, and she was surprised that I could remember it, as I was not quite three years old, when he died in April 1955. In this memory, many of his ten children and their families were gathered around his sick bed. My parents, sister and I had traveled from Chicago back to Ohio on the B & O (Baltimore & Ohio) Railway to visit him, and this was the last time we saw him alive. I was standing at his right shoulder when he reached around and handed me a small brown paper bag full of Super Bubble pieces—the bubble-gum in the red, blue and yellow wrapper with the two twisted ends. He had brown eyes and a pleasant smile. My mother was standing near his right foot and she seemed pleased at this quiet, simple exchange.

***

We stayed at North Pine Grove until a fire destroyed our apartment building in the summer of 1958. It was started in the "English basement" apartment adjacent to ours and was caused by a cigarette smoldering on the couch. The sleeping smoker miraculously awoke and ran out into the hallway yelling "fire," awakening my parents.

My sister and I were sleeping in the locked front apartment. Our bedroom door was also locked on the *outside*, as my father had put a lock on the door so that they could lock us in there whenever they took

81

a notion to be rid of us for awhile. He unlocked the bedroom door and roused Esther and me from our sleep, then led us out into the hallway where the smoke was so thick I couldn't see my hand in front of my face. Not being able to see, we groped along to find and follow the walls, but soon found that they were red hot to the touch. We also quickly found out that it was impossible to draw in even a tiny breath without breaking into spasms of coughing.

My father told us, "hold your breath; move as fast as you can." He led us through the hallway to the back of the building where there was an exit to the alley. My mother was already outside waiting for us; we were the first ones out. Then my father went back inside the building to awaken others.

Soon people came running out of the flaming building into the night, filling the streets and alley. Standing outside in the alley, I turned and looked back up at the building. Jagged red-orange flames from the back porches of several stories of apartments were stabbing the night sky.

The red fire trucks soon came roaring up the narrow street from the historic Wrigleyville station on Waveland Avenue. We stood outside in our pajamas watching the firemen unload huge hoses from the truck, aim the nozzles and fire hundreds of gallons of splashing water at the sizzling, smoldering building. Other firemen on ladders crashed through windows and rescued many terrified residents through the jagged glass holes of upper-level apartments.

All of us residents standing in the street and alley were instantly homeless. No one could go back inside the building. That night, in our pajamas, we went to the home of a church family, and stayed with them until we found another place to live.

Several days later, residents were allowed to reenter the building to reclaim personal property. We filed along the same basement hallway through which several days earlier we'd staggered, as in a bad dream, out of the burning building. It was dark and eerie, there was no electricity in the building, the walls were charred and scarred, and there was the debris of stairs, walls, and columns that had been axed down by the firemen. There was water all over the floors and the whole place reeked of moldy smoke.

We crept back into the front apartment where my sister and I had slept, and into the kitchen, and there we heard one surrealistic, faint chirp. We looked at each other in pleasant amazement. The night of the fire, as every night before going to bed, my mother had covered the bird cage and set it down on the floor under the kitchen table.

We quickly yanked the birdcage out from under the table and snatched off the cover and there were our parakeets, Salt and Pepper. They seemed quite their typical selves, nonchalant and unharmed. No one could explain how these birds had survived the fire. Perhaps they lived because my mother had covered the cage and slid it safely under the table, and because we'd closed the apartment door leading out to the smoky hallway behind us, as we evacuated the burning building that night.

***

Things seemed to accelerate downhill after my mother's father died in April 1955. She was institutionalized shortly thereafter, and Esther and I were made wards of the state and placed in foster care by our legal guardian, the Evangelical Child Welfare Agency, 127 North Dearborn Street, Chicago.

83

Esther and I were later returned to our parents on North Pine Grove, and I attended kindergarten in 1957, the year of *Sputnik I*, at nearby LeMoyne School. On my first report card, the teacher wrote that I showed special interest in books and art.

Then we moved northwest and stayed in a two different apartments near D.R. Cameron School, which is still at Grand and Monticello. Those apartments were mice-, roach-, and rat-infested, in a neighborhood not nearly as nice as North Pine Grove.

By this time my grandfather may have cut off financial support to my father, who had so quickly acquiesced to yet another failure, that of flunking out of Moody Bible Institute.

He took various unskilled jobs at such places as Quaker Rubber Corporation and later the National Bedding Company, staying at each place of employ until he got into an argument with someone, or until he had a seizure on the job, after which he was predictably fired. Always suspicious, he was not able to get along with anyone, and accused anyone and everyone of this or that wrong against him.

I remember my mother telling me that he lost his job at Quaker Rubber because he'd accused his boss of "deliberately trying to kill him," after his boss assigned him to a job requiring him to be up on a lift. I distinctly remember the exasperation in my mother's voice when she said, "Can you imagine him believing his boss actually tried to kill him?"

One Christmas all employees at his plant received gifts. Somehow his gift was a carton of Camel cigarettes; we could smell the fresh tobacco even before he opened it. My mother, noting the disgusted look on my father's face as he sat unwrapping the gift, asked, "Well, why don't you just give them to someone else who smokes?"

He answered her with grave seriousness that was

ridiculous even to me at the age of six. "No," he said, I won't do that because "these cigarettes have been poisoned." My mother and I looked at each other in horror at his suggestion; we knew he wasn't referring to nicotine or carbon monoxide.

Then he had me accompany him down to the furnace room in the basement of the apartment building where he unlatched the huge wrought-iron furnace door; letting it cautiously creak open. Then with ceremonious piety he tossed the cigarettes into the flames, slammed the door shut, and flipped over the latch with a flourish.

9. Division Street between Hamlin and Avers

After the fire on North Pine Grove, we moved to a third-floor flat at 3915 West Division Street, just east of Pulaski Road, and a few blocks west of the Division Street and Grand Avenue intersection. There was a small playground adjacent to our small, three-flat building and we were within walking distance to D.R. Cameron School.

During this time, my mother became pregnant and even more withdrawn than usual. When she was quite visibly pregnant she took to her bedroom and I didn't see her for weeks. One day she came out of the bedroom and I noticed she was not wearing her usual marble-green maternity outfit, the only maternity apparel she had. I could see she was no longer pregnant, and I asked her tentatively, "What happened to you?"

"I lost the baby, I miscarried." she spat out in a fierce whisper.

Knowing that she hadn't been out of the bedroom for weeks, I pressed, "You mean you lost the baby in the bed?"

"Yes."

"How's that?" It was always difficult to get her to talk about anything.

"Because I fell."

I was so curious and filled with questions, but I knew she'd clam up at any time, so I asked carefully, "Where is the baby?"

"Your father flushed it down the toilet."

I felt my scalp crawl. "What did the baby look like? Was it developed?" I couldn't believe my boldness.

"Oh yes, fully developed; you could see everything, its fingers and toes, everything. It was a boy."
She said this in a distant voice, without any emotion.
"Did you go to the doctor?"
"No," she answered blankly.

***

My parents argued increasingly about their lack of money. As children, each of them had been accustomed to abundance; they had never experienced poverty, or even observed it in others. Their arguing vexed me greatly, and as I was an intelligent and intuitive child, I was keenly aware of our desperate situation.

One Saturday morning, when I was seven years old, I got the idea to pay a visit to Mrs. Flynn next door. Mrs. Flynn was regarded with curiosity by my parents. "She's divorced," as my mother told me in a whisper. She had red hair, smoked cigarettes constantly, and was employed. She was raising a son and a daughter, both teenagers. Compared to us, she seemed to have enough money. They always seemed to have plenty to eat and all wore decent clothes, though certainly it was true that she was not wealthy. She greeted me pleasantly and let me into her apartment, which was also on the third floor.

"Can we borrow some money?" I asked bluntly.

"What do you mean? What for?"

"For food, we don't have anything to eat." She eyed me curiously, but seemed to trust me.

"How much do you want?"

I hadn't expected that question. "Whatever you can give," I said.

She went into the kitchen and rummaged through

88

a large purse, pulling out a white pack of Kent cigarettes, and then an overstuffed wallet. She unsnapped the strap and peered inside. I saw many dollars; she handed me three. I was quite satisfied because I thought this was a large sum of money.

"Thank-you, thank-you" I said, embarrassed and not knowing what else to say.

I was eager to go to my parents and present them with the money. I wanted so badly to make them happy. As usual, however, I approached my parents with great fear and caution.

Later that evening, I managed to say, "There's something I want to tell you." I was stammering, and I could hardly get the words out. For some reason this got my father's attention and he became impatient and agitated. I started to panic since my plan wasn't turning out as I'd hoped. This was supposed to make them happy, but it wasn't, and I felt my nerve slipping. I continued to panic and even wished I hadn't borrowed the money from Mrs. Flynn or approached my parents.

In an instant my father was enraged. Even though this was characteristic of him, it was always confusing and terrifying to me. He yanked off his belt with a flourish, as he always did, and began to beat me. I fell to the floor and the three dollars that I hadn't even gotten the chance to offer him, fluttered down around us. My father was stunned for a few seconds; he looked at the money, and then at my mother with amazement and curiosity. She stood by quietly, showing no emotion.

"Where did you get this?" he raged, grabbing me by the shirt, his putrid breath in my face. He began to beat me again with his belt; he was clearly out of control.

My sister began to scream and cry in response to the violence, adding to the crazy chaos. She was always quick to scream or cry, and strangely that never seemed to provoke my father. I could hardly speak and he continued to roar and lash out at me with his belt. My mother stood by quietly, never coming to my defense.

"Mrs. Flynn," I finally managed to get out.

He stopped and glared down at me on the floor. Then he abruptly turned and left the apartment, leaving me astonished and trembling on the floor.

I never heard anymore from him about the incident. Several days later, I tentatively asked my mother what he did with the money. She said he went to Mrs. Flynn who confirmed my story. My mother said that we needed the money and so he kept it, but paid Mrs. Flynn back on his next payday. After all I went through to try to get us some food, I noticed that he didn't buy groceries with the money.

***

It was while we lived at the apartment on Division Street, that Pepper, the blue parakeet, died. I was at the small playground, next to our apartment building and happened to notice my father come outside from the back door. He'd jogged down two flights of stairs from our third-floor apartment, which let out onto a large landing covered with asphalt shingles. This landing had a banister around it and was actually the roof of the first-floor apartment below.

I watched him walk across the asphalt shingles with quick, crackling footsteps, sounding like he was walking on sticky tiles of tacky tar. He moved swiftly and deliberately to the other side and down a flight of stairs to the alley. He was carrying a small bundle of wrapped newspaper.

Later, when I came inside and noticed that Pepper the parakeet was missing from the cage, I realized that what I'd seen earlier was him carrying the dead bird out to the garbage cans in the alley. The bird hadn't been sick that I knew of. When I'd gone outside to play, the birds were chirping to each other, but now Pepper was gone. Neither of our parents gave any words of explanation nor comfort about our pet's death, and the incident left me with an eerie and ominous mood of fear.

***

On December 1, 1958 there was a horrific fire at nearby Our Lady of Angels Roman Catholic School, 909 North Avers Avenue. My mother reported the events to me in gory detail. The fire started in a garbage drum in the basement. Light fixtures and transom windows exploded as the fire broke through the roof. Before evacuation equipment arrived, students leapt from the windows. Ninety students and three nuns were trapped and died on the top floor of Our Lady of Angels School while Engine 85 was mistakenly directed to Our Lady of Angels Church, around the corner on Iowa Street. Their smothering and burning deaths were terrifying to me, as I vividly recalled the fire we'd experienced just a year earlier on North Pine Grove Avenue.

From then on, my sister would not sleep by herself, and every night after they were asleep, she crept from her bed into my parent's bed where she slept for the rest of the night. She was indulged and allowed to stay with them, but I was ordered to stay in my bed. I was afraid to sleep in the back bedroom alone because it seemed so far away from the front bedroom where my parents and Esther slept.

I was also afraid of rats. One night, my fear near-ly overwhelming me, I asked my father, "Do you think the rats can get into my bed?" I desperately wanted him to assure me that they couldn't. But he wouldn't answer me and therefore I knew that they could.

My bed was on a metal frame several inches above the floor, and lying in my bed alone in the dark I tried to comfort myself. I reasoned that the rats couldn't climb up the legs of a metal frame. But the cloth-cov-ered box springs sat directly on the narrow metal frame and I knew the rats could easily dig their claws into the fabric and get right into my bed. I remem-bered a story my mother had told me about rats get-ting into a crib and eating the baby alive. I huddled in the center of my bed unable to sleep, worried that I'd be awakened to the horror of a rat gnawing on my face.

By this time, I began to have nightmares. The cumulative effect of my many anxieties started to pile up in my psyche. The incident with my mother and her miscarriage, the flushing of the baby down the toilet, the unmentioned and un-grieved death of our parakeet, the fires, our extreme poverty, and my father's cruelty were all bad enough, but the most frightening was that I could read my parents well and I was acutely aware that we were in a desperate situ-ation. They were overwhelmed.

I was burdened with worry about everything, as a child. I had the intelligence and the sensitivity to fig-ure things out, but I didn't have the emotional where-withal to reassure myself. I knew too much for my age, and my parents did nothing to reassure me that we were going to be okay.

Quite the opposite: they shared every doubt, fear, and insecurity, casting all their negative thoughts onto me. Consequently, I never had a truly carefree moment in my childhood, not a one. Every minute of my childhood was filled with worry, anxiety, insecurity and even terror.

Amazingly I did well in school, because school was a refuge and a haven for me. I was at Cameron School in the classroom or on the playground every minute that I could be. At school, I was relaxed and distracted from my wretched home life.

Just after my mother's miscarriage, I had anxiety-type dreams which I still remember. The most frightening dream took place at a totally benign and nondescript building which I walked past on my way to and from school every day.

In my dream, as I approached the building, I heard agonizing screams and moans from many children. I could see in the front windows that unknown adults were holding the children down against their will and were dismembering them alive. Next, I realized in terror that the murderers inside had noticed me walking past, so they ran outside and started chasing me down the street. I started running but a strong wind was holding me back. The murderers were quickly catching up with me, and were going to dismember me in the same fashion that I'd observed them do to the other children.

This dream nearly incapacitated me with terror, and I was ashamed about that. I didn't dare talk to anyone about it because I'd learned early on to keep everything to myself. But as days, then weeks went by, the dream stayed with me and I became utterly terrified, anxious, and depressed. I tried hard to forget the nightmare and go on. Even at age seven, I knew realistically that it "was just a dream," but I just couldn't reassure myself. Being at school did help, but I had to walk back and forth past the building of my nightmare scenario every day.

My mother was not available; she was always

behind closed doors and I never told her anything anyway. Finally though, I became desperate. I knew that if I could have just a little bit of help in the way of a sense of security, I could get through it. I desperately wished for just a little bit of time in a safe space, and an adult's reassurance.

I felt like I was alone in the world; I could see that my parents were totally unable to take care of me in any way, especially comfort me, because they were not able to do these things for themselves. Not only were they unable to care for my physical and emotional needs, but they were to be feared and avoided as they continually caused me mental and physical pain. Understanding that my parents were my enemies was terrifying for me to know, but I knew it from my earliest recollection.

In desperation, I asked my father, as casually as I could, if someone could walk with me to school, "just for a few days," I pleaded.

"What do you mean someone walk with you to school?" he scoffed.

"Like Mom, or Mrs. Flynn, just for a few days?" I didn't dare tell him why, even though the terror of the dream was still fresh.

He looked at me curiously, "Are you kidding? Your mother can't walk to school with you, and Mrs. Flynn works. There is no one to walk to school with you. You will walk to school by yourself like you always have. I walk to my job. Who do you think you are? What kind of crap is this, anyway?" His voice escalated in anger; there was no compassion and no reassurance. He didn't ask me whether there was a problem, or whether something was wrong. My request had only incurred his wrath and scorn.

I was crushed and even more terrified. At seven years old, I didn't think I could carry on. It is hard for most of us to imagine a depressed child. Children are usually spontaneous, have short memories, and think only of their next pleasure. They believe that their parents and the whole world exist only for their immediate gratification. I have never known any of that. A depressed child is beaten down in spirit, withdrawn, anxious, nervous, and too afraid even to cry. I was beaten down and haunted with fear and I rarely had a spontaneously happy moment as a child.

I had another nightmare which had as the setting the Elm-LaSalle Bible Church that my father was attending at the time. I dreamed that some adults were burying me alive under the flooring in one of the hallways of the church basement. They were doing this against my protests, and very slowly I was suffocating to death. I awoke, my heart pounding in terror, and was gasping for breath, "suffocating" just as in the dream. The details of the dream were explicit, such as the location in the church, and the sounds of the men ripping up the linoleum flooring to bury me, and the lid of the coffin slamming down inches above my nose.

These dreams were the result of the suppressed, intense anxiety that I, as a seven-year-old girl, felt as a result of knowing from my earliest self-awareness that I was completely alone in this world—there was no one to love and comfort me. This knowing was mostly intuitive and subconscious, and I could not have articulated my feelings.

I now realize that the themes of these nightmares reveal my excruciating anxiety as a child, and that they may also have been the result of some earlier trauma known only to my subconscious mind. My parents were not only useless to me, but harmful. This danger made my childhood nearly unbearable, full of fear, terror, depression, wariness and existential loneliness.

10. Lawndale at Grand

We had moved from the apartment on Division near Pulaski Road, to 1228 North Lawndale, a side street near the corner of Grand, directly across from the playground of D.R. Cameron School. Both apartments were within walking distance to Cameron School. So, I told my teachers that I was going home for lunch, but I went hunting for empty bottles in the alleys and on the playground. There was never any lunch at home.

I was always hungry; each day was a new challenge to find something to eat. This was primary reality for me, the first thing on my mind from my earliest recollection until I was placed in the Children's Home, where, though not fancy by any means, we always had plenty to eat. I never recall my mother cooking a meal, much less going to the grocery store; she almost never left the house.

I collected pop bottles daily from the playground across the street and the adjacent alley so that I could return them to the neighborhood grocery store for pennies. When we lived on Lawndale Avenue, across the street from the large playground at Cameron School, it was pretty easy to find several bottles a day. There were no cans or disposable plastic bottles in those days. I could get two pennies for each bottle returned.

Much of the candy at the store was priced at two pieces for a penny and I was careful to select the largest pieces, or the candy that would take the longest time to consume. For example, a pretzel log lasted a long time. I licked off the salt first, and then like an edentulous baby, I gummed the pretzel trying to make it last as long as possible. I never allowed

97

myself the luxury of gobbling up food with hearty abandon. I was never sure when I'd get my next bite to eat.

We didn't go to Wrigley Field often because my father couldn't afford it, but he enjoyed baseball and so we went a few times. He never bought snacks for us though, ostensibly because he couldn't afford both snacks and the admission. I watched others eating hot dogs, popcorn, and peanuts. I picked up the peanut shells that others threw on the ground, and I ate them. They were salty and tasty and filling, and I was hungry. I picked up as many as I could when my father wasn't looking and put them in my pocket, saving them to eat later.

If I was really hungry, I went door to door in the neighborhood begging for food. I simply rang the bell, and asked the person who opened it, "Do you have anything to eat?" Most adults eyed me curiously, but then turned and left me standing at their open front door, where I gazed inside at what always seemed to me to be opulent living conditions.

Soon the stranger returned with a cookie or a piece of candy. It occurred to me even then, that the people didn't believe I was truly hungry, but thought instead that, like any other child, I just wanted some sweets. Once in a while someone slammed the door in my face.

I had about as many school pals as I wanted and frequently went with them to their homes for lunch or after school, staying away from my parent's apartment as much as possible. I always hoped that their mother would offer us something to eat and she always did—a baloney sandwich on Wonder bread, Jay's potato chips, Hostess Twinkies, chocolate cupcakes or cookies, and always milk. My classmates all seemed to have plenty to eat, a modest but comfortable place to live, and a nice mother.

Over the years, it's occurred to me that my parents weren't so poor that they couldn't have done a better job providing food for us. My father could have had his financial priorities straight and my mother could have prepared something for us. He had no ability to manage money, and was deliberately cruel, delighting in withholding food from us when we were hungry. Many times I begged my parents for food.

My mother seemed utterly lazy to me, and so totally in her own world; she was always locked behind a closed door, always in her bedroom. She had no ability to recognize and respond to the needs and emotions of her children or anyone else.

However, like most people, she could go out and accomplish something when she really wanted to. For example, in one of the few times I remember her going outside, she walked more than a mile from our apartment at 1228 North Lawndale to a pawn shop on North Avenue and pawned her wedding rings.

The rings were my father's mother's wedding rings. She certainly didn't stop and buy any groceries with the money on her way home. I'm sure she didn't pawn the rings to buy baloney sandwiches for us, but to spite my father for something. As soon as he found out about it, he and I walked quickly to the pawn shop and got the rings back. He was surprisingly calm and deliberate but the tension was palpable.

Even then, I realized she must have been unspeakably angry at him to pawn his deceased mother's wedding rings. That or else she was so utterly mentally incompetent as not to realize the immeasurable sentimental value of her wedding rings, the rings that Forest Hall had given to his soon-to-be-deceased bride Esther, and that were then given in marriage to Joy, by Esther's only surviving, adoring son Paul.

***

We didn't have a cafeteria at D.R. Cameron School, and certainly not soft drink or snack machines. At lunchtime, the kids went home if they lived very close, or else they ate their sack lunches in the basement, sitting at long wooden tables and benches, eating sandwiches and cookies.

I don't remember my mother cooking a meal and our family sitting down at the table to eat. I used to wonder how my sister got enough to eat. Many years later, I had the chance to compare hers and my recollections of our common childhood experience of continuous gnawing hunger. She told me that at times, she ate paste, crayons and bird seed.

"Esther, I've always wondered where you got your food."

She answered without hesitation, "Oh, I went to the Jewel every day and stole something to eat."

"You what?" I exclaimed. "What do you mean? You stole food?"

"Oh, sure I did. I walked up and down the aisles and picked out anything and everything I wanted to eat, and then I simply walked out of the store with it. Nobody ever stopped me or said anything to me about it."

I was amazed. "Weren't you afraid you'd get caught?"

"No. I was hungry."

***

100

Once I asked my father for fifty cents for a subscription to *The Weekly Reader*, a children's newspaper, which is still distributed at school today. He hollered at me, "Someone is always begging me for money," then he cursed my teacher. He never gave me the money, and I was ashamed to tell the teacher that my father wouldn't pay for my subscription. Along with all my classmates, however, the teacher always gave me my very own *Weekly Reader*, even though I hadn't paid for it, and also a carton of milk each morning, both of which I devoured.

Another time, I got up the courage to ask my father for a bicycle. He blasted at me, "No!" Soon after, I noticed that he bought a bicycle for himself and began riding it to work. He wouldn't let me ride it though, not once.

Every winter the fireman came and with huge hoses they flooded the playground at Cameron School, making a skating rink for the kids. I watched the skaters enviously day after day. It looked so graceful and fun; and I wanted to try it too. For Christmas, I begged my father for a pair of ice skates.

He gave me a pair of men's black hockey skates several sizes too large. They were not wrapped, not in a box and they were considerably worn.

"Mom, where did he get these skates?"

"From the Goodwill," she said flatly.

I was hurt, but not at all surprised at the inappropriateness of his gift because this kind of behavior from him was not unusual. The skates were much too big, but I very much wanted to skate, so I put on many pairs of socks and taught myself to skate on them, and used them for a couple of winters.

***

I avoided home as much as possible. I was terrified of my father, and I didn't want to be around my mother as she had become increasingly distant, unpredictable, even cursing and lashing out in anger at me, which was utterly out of character for her.

One evening after school, I complained to her that I was hungry. She had been sitting quietly, staring blankly into space as though deep in thought. She got up and went into the kitchen; I heard her rummaging through a kitchen drawer. I thought she was going to prepare something to eat. Thinking this pleasantly curious, I walked towards the kitchen door to see what she could have found to for us to eat. She spun around and came at me with a carving knife in her hand. I'll never forget the look on her face as she came toward me holding the knife in her fist, the tip pointed downward.

For a few seconds, I was stunned and confused but soon I turned and ran into the bedroom and scurried under the bed, figuring that she would not be able to reach me there. I could see her feet as she stood quietly for a few moments breathing heavily through her teeth.

I lay under the box spring which was held up by the metal frame and studied the wood slats just under the sheer fabric covering them. The label on the underside of the box spring read: manufactured at National Bedding Corporation, Fullerton Avenue, Chicago.

My heart was pounding in terror and confusion as I lay as quietly as I could, as close to the wall and as far away from the edge of the bed as possible. *Geez, what in the world is wrong with her now?* As I huddled close to the wall, I calculated that the knife blade was not long enough to penetrate through both the mattress and box spring and sure hoped that I wouldn't have to find out I was wrong about that.

Finally, I heard her feet, in the worn, pink rubber flip-flops, shuffle away.

I thought about the window on the same wall as the head of the bed. I remembered that it was easy to open and that there was no screen on it. There was no sound for a long time and I wondered *where did she go, what's she doing now?* I scooted on the floor toward the edge of the bed and peered out into the room.

Then in one second I was out from under the bed and on my feet. I quickly flipped the small lock on top of the bare window frame, and flung the window wide open. With agility and ease, I tumbled out of our first floor apartment window and jumped down into the gangway. I stayed outside at the playground across the street until dusk, at which time I knew I'd have to go back because my father would expect me to be home, or else.

***

I used to walk the eight or more blocks north to the Springfield Tank, on Springfield Avenue at Wabansia, where kids could swim for free. I had to cross the large intersection of North Avenue near Pulaski, but even at age eight I walked this round trip myself. It was a large indoor public swimming pool; the walls were dull gray tiles. The echo factor in there was incredible, and it was always noisy with so many kids.

I remember having another nightmare about a man lurking in one of the many entry ways along North Avenue and grabbing me as I walked by to the Springfield Tank. This again had the same effect as the earlier dreams and again I was afraid to walk out-

103

side alone, though maybe this was not such an irrational fear. But I very much wanted to go swimming and there was no one to walk with me, so I "got over it" and walked the roughly two miles one way, to the Springfield Tank and back by myself.

There was also a small YMCA at the corner of Lawndale and Grand where I learned to shoot pool and play ping pong. They often bused us kids into the city to larger YMCA facilities, with a pool.

Once a week after school, the buses were parked at the curb on Lawndale facing Grand Avenue, waiting to load us kids, boys and girls, and take us to a larger YMCA, where there was a swimming pool. I remember this was a long, circuitous bus ride; and at night it was difficult to know where we were going, but it seemed to me we were heading in a mostly easterly direction. I knew that I wasn't entirely sure where I was, and this made me a little uneasy.

To this day I'm not sure where that YMCA was, and more than that my parents had no idea where we went either, though they never asked. But we kids were well supervised and fortunately there were never any problems.

We swam hard; by that time, at eight years old, I was doing forwards and backwards flips off the diving boards. I wore myself out swimming lap after lap, even though I knew I'd suffer screaming leg aches that night.

The bus ride home was fun in the dark, cozy bus and we were all pleasantly exhausted. All the kids brought forth grease splotched, brown bag sack lunches stuffed with chocolate cream-filled Hostess cupcakes, or Twinkies, and thick baloney or tuna sandwiches, the mayonnaise oozing out the sides as they bit into them, lunches their mothers had prepared for them.

They ate nonchalantly, bantering among themselves and eating without a care in the world. I watched them and marveled at how they could eat so slowly, how they could even bother to talk and socialize, instead of just gobbling up their food, which is what I wanted to do. I could hardly stand to watch them; I was starving but had no lunch of my own to eat.

Despite my constant hunger, I was blessed with robust health and played very hard outside. However, from earliest recollection, I had frequent and severe leg aches which hurt mostly at night and would cause searing pain. I could hardly hold still or keep from crying out, the pain was so bad. My parents acted as though they didn't believe I was in pain, as though I was faking it. They would ignore me, or lock me up in the bedroom.

My father would taunt me saying, "If you have such terrible leg aches, you need to rest."

I remember my father had put outside locks on our bedroom door and whenever he took a notion to be rid of me, such as when I got leg aches, or on a Sunday afternoon, he locked me in my bedroom. Now, of course, I realize what they were doing on Sunday afternoons. Being locked in the bedroom always scared the wits out of me though, especially after the fire on North Pine Grove as there was a lock on our bedroom door there too.

I was filled with terror, anger, helplessness, and panic when I heard the door lock, and I begged and pleaded with him not to lock me in the room, but he always did it without a moment's hesitation, without saying a word, completely ignoring my pleas. I moaned for hours, rubbing my legs and rolling around on the bed.

***

Luckily we lived across the street from Cameron School and I could easily be there all the time. I loved school and devoured all the books and class materials I could get my hands on. I enjoyed all subjects including math and science but excelled in the verbal skills. There was no subject I didn't like; I liked reading, math, science, history, geography, spelling, drama and acting, music—everything.

In the third grade, all of us were given the Sanford-Binet IQ test. I was found to be reading at more than three grade levels higher, and was significantly above average in all subjects. This news surprised me because I made no special effort and I certainly was not tutored or encouraged by my parents or anyone else to excel.

I remember that my teacher, the principal, and the assistant principal made a big issue of this, as my scores were the highest in the class, "The highest we've ever seen." But I could not share in their celebration and the more they praised me, the more uneasy I became because I knew exactly how my father would react.

The school officials contacted my parents for a conference and recommended that I be double promoted. My father flatly refused, saying that I would "get too big of a head, get too big for my britches," and that I "should be kept equal" with my younger sister, who failed math repeatedly and did not get good grades. So I wasn't double promoted, and I was overtly discouraged academically, "so that Esther's feelings wouldn't be hurt," as my mother later explained it to me.

With academics my father tried very hard to create sibling rivalry between us, and it worked because I strongly resented being held back to Esther's level and constantly being compared with her. I was always striving or begging for something or another, or working hard to receive some privilege, only to see it then automatically and easily handed to her. I often got punished and beaten up while Esther "got away with murder," because she was emotionally and physically frail, petite, and feminine. I knew well that she was my father's mother's namesake and also resembled his mother Esther, whom he worshipped.

I knew I was vastly different from my sister in many significant ways. I wanted to be me, and I did not want her to be me. I hated it when on a few occasions we were dressed in matching clothes. I wanted each of us to be accepted as the vastly different individuals that we are.

He made it very clear to me that he would not tolerate any smartness out of me, and that also meant any scholastic excelling.

Even though my parents were inattentive and negligent, they already knew before my test scores that I had a superior intelligence. When I was three years old and we lived at the North Pine Grove apartment, I was in the kitchen with my mother, sitting on the floor with crayons and paper. I was amusing myself with writing the letters of the alphabet; then I printed my name, and the names of my sister, mother and father. My mother happened to glance at what I was doing and she acted astonished, even alarmed. She hurriedly turned off the kitchen faucets and dried her hands.

She grabbed the paper from me asking in an accusing voice, "How long have you been doing this?" Within the interior world of a three-year-old, it seemed I had been writing for as long as I could remember and I didn't think it was any big deal. My mother kept the paper; she said she was going to show it my father when he came home from work. I hoped that didn't mean I was going to get beaten. When he saw it that evening, he dated it, and filed it a particular manila file folder in his oak file cabinet, slammed the drawer with a flourish, but never said a word to me about it.

Over the years I came to realize that it was better to hide my voracious reading and my insatiable curiosity, and I always did. I was very careful to keep my mouth shut and always appear dumb, especially dumber than my father.

***

At Cameron School, there was an active Club House on the playground, where kids of all ages hung around, as the school was for kindergarten through the twelfth grade. There was a juke box, ping pong tables, pool tables, baseballs, bats, softballs, foot-balls, volleyballs, and other game equipment like a floor hopscotch game which was played inside with a pink rubber ball.

Outside there were several variations of "monkey bar" sets on the playground and a softball field. I was extremely athletic and coordinated as a child. I played hard and rough—softball, volleyball, and I mastered all the playground equipment. The Club House was open every afternoon and evening with adult attendants; most neighbor kids spent a lot of time there, especially me. After dusk, the floodlights were turned on, illuminating the entire playground and Club House area. The juke box played endlessly, such songs as the "Peppermint Twist," by Joey Dee and the Starlighters, "The Wanderer," by Dion, and "The Lion Sleeps Tonight" by the Tokens. Kids would spontaneously begin dancing to the music, lining up to do the Stroll when "Duke of Earl," by Gene Chandler, came on.

What a fascinating and distracting world of self-confident, fearless children this Chicago schoolyard was. Then here was the bottomless pop machine, though it was mostly the teenagers who had dimes to put into it. Many times they'd leave their Cokes or orange drinks half consumed. I'd secretly pick up the discarded pop bottles from the wooden racks and drink up the remains. I thoroughly enjoyed being at the school during the day and at the Club House in the evenings. My father said I had to be home "by dark" but I soon learned that the definition of dark was simply when he said it was.

***

One Friday night, when I was in the third grade, there was a Science Fair at school. I had no money for any materials to make a science project, but I'd seen the "egg in the bottle" trick and was fascinated with the explanation. I figured I could come up with a glass quart milk bottle, one egg, and some matches. I had practiced making a small fire in the bottle, and then setting the peeled boiled egg, small end down, on the mouth of the bottle. Within a few seconds, the fire went out, and then with a resonant kerplunk, the egg was sucked down, intact, into the bottle.

I had thought a lot about my science project and mentally rehearsed my presentation for weeks. I planned to ask passers-by at the science fair if they knew how to get the egg into the bottle without smashing it. Then with a sense of mystery, I had planned to light the fire in the bottle, set the egg on the rim and watch their eyes as the egg was soon sucked into the bottle. Then I planned to explain

109

with great erudition that nature abhors a vacuum; that the fire consumed the oxygen, creating a vacuum in the milk bottle and so the pressure outside of the bottle was greater than the pressure inside, and so the egg was pushed (not sucked) into the bottle.

The whole science fair plan was so exciting and what's more, my father promised he'd come. When the Friday night finally came, we students set up our science projects in the hallway of the school. As it got late, I kept watching the front door looking for my father. He never showed up. Finally all the kids packed up their projects and left the school with their parents. I walked across the playground to our apartment on Lawndale, a small street just across from the school. My father was home playing with a new reel-to-reel Weber tape recorder that he'd just bought on his way home from work with his weekly Friday pay.

"Did you forget the Science Fair tonight?" I asked timidly. I was sure he'd rage at me and slug me in the face.

"Oh that," he mumbled. He didn't even look up; he was too engrossed and delighted with his new toy.

It took at least a couple of weeks paychecks to pay for that tape recorder. In time to come, I saw that his primary interest in the tape recorder was so that he could surreptitiously tape arguments with my mother. He'd hide the tape behind a chair and put in on "record." Then he'd goad my mother into an argument, which was easy for him to do. He was trying to collect incriminating evidence he thought he needed to prove she was insane. I could see that he thought this the most delightful sport of all, and the tape recorder was his favorite gadget for all the rest of the years I knew of him

110

Buttermilk at Room Temp

I taste it with memory's mouth
warm liquid velvet
makes a sour mustache
push it through my teeth
warm milk on my gums
feels like lowering into a bath.
Relax my little-boy jaw
sticky rivulets down my neck
running stream back into time
to sticky tickly in my infant ears.
Once I was one of 36 sturdy wooden desks
the blackboards were really black;
by mid-morning the room was tropical.
A tall large-faced fan
watched us from the corner.
The humming hot air
was hypnotic because
I was hungry, really hungry.
A muscular man in dark green work clothes,
his gloves delivered a square meshed
wire basket of milk cartons.
I dozed and dreamed of the sweating cartons
and could think of nothing else
save that one would soon be mine.
So when the time finally came round again
I who nursed only at school
remember that the milk was room temp
thick like abundant, sour like rich
because I was hungry, really hungry.

***

When I was about eight years old I came down with some illness that I just couldn't shake and I was ashamed about that. I was fatigued and constantly nauseated for weeks, and I finally became so worried that I got up the courage to mention my symptoms to my mother. When my father got home from work, they both began to mock me and jeer at me. Never before had both of them ganged up on me at the same time; and feeling weak, this surprised me and caught me off guard.

My mother was pregnant again, this time with my brother Larry, and they both started in on me, "What's the matter with you, do you think you're pregnant too? You're not the pregnant one here, your mother is."

What a cruel and inappropriate thing for them to say to an eight-year-old girl, and I was crushed.

I sure tried but couldn't will myself to get well. After several weeks, and at the intervention of my school teacher, my father in a huff and complaining all the way about what "this was going to cost me" took me to see a physician. By this time I was utterly weak in body and in spirit. My teachers had apparently noticed that I'd lost weight, was withdrawn, and had been mute for some time. I sat in the doctor's office waiting for our turn, but was so weak I could hardly sit up.

Finally, we were ushered into the examining room. The doctor was graying, soft-spoken, and serious. He took my hand as I stepped up onto the stepstool. I couldn't hoist myself up and so he lifted me up onto the table. My father silently stood by. The doctor began to speak softly to me, trying patiently to get me to talk, but I couldn't even make eye contact with him. I noticed the nurse in her white uniform, white cap, shoes, and stockings busying herself with her back to us. Then she turned and faced the doctor; they communicated something to each other with their eyes. The doctor then asked my father to leave the room. He looked startled, but left as requested. Then both the doctor and the nurse pulled up chairs and sat beside me. Looking up at me sitting on the examining table, they began to talk lovingly and encouraged me to tell them "what was wrong." They began to ask probing questions. I just couldn't speak, even with my father out of the room. I was too over-whelmed, too weak and dispirited. But I began to cry and sob with great release and sadness; the first time I remember crying in my life, as crying would have resulted in my father's fist in my face. The doctor then took me onto his lap and held me tenderly, like a true father, while I cried my heart out. The nurse watched on patiently, stroking my hair. I'll never for-get the kindness of this nurse and physician.

I was diagnosed with pneumonia and admitted to Augustana Hospital, and stayed for a week. To me, it seemed like being at a luxurious hotel. I had three huge meals of any food I wanted. Everyone who took care of me was cheerful, friendly and kind and I was not at all afraid of being there by myself. The only unpleasant thing was that I was given a shot of peni-cillin twice a day in the butt.

***

Learning the Thunder

Fortunately, since my father couldn't drive, Chicago public transportation was quite accessible even in the 1950's. He was proud of his ability to use varying combinations of public transportation and to travel easily and anywhere he wanted to go the city.

113

My mother almost never left our apartment but I went everywhere with him, even a couple of times to the furniture and bedding company where he worked. I think he was trying very hard to have a happy life, even if his wife wouldn't join in with him, and that was one reason why I was his constant companion.

We went everywhere together: to Wrigley Field to see the Cubs play; to Soldier's Field to see the fireworks; to Moody Memorial Church; to Lake Michigan for fishing; and to the tennis courts at Lincoln and Humbolt Parks where he taught me how to play tennis. I still have his old wooden tennis racket from his youth and the one he bought for my mother. One time we went to Riverview, the famous amusement park at Belmont and Western, and rode the Fireball roller coaster together.

While riding the CTA bus, he'd sit next to the window with his foot propped up on the ledge above the heater vents along the floor. He'd write poetry on scraps of paper which he balanced on his knee. He'd sit as in a trance, staring blankly ahead; then after a time he'd gleefully exclaim, "I got it," and scribble some words with his pencil. Writing poetry seemed to make him happy and he seemed to take pride in his collection of original poems. He wrote scores of poems, probably hundreds by this time; and he typed them on onionskin paper, hunting and pecking on an old gray Royal typewriter. Then he put them in order and bound them in a light gray, soft cover folder.

As a kid I secretly read most all his poems; I recall that I was impressed with his technical ability, though not interested his mostly religious themes, which I thought were overly self-righteous, sappy, and archaic sounding. However one of his poems, "Two Little Girls with Cute Little Curls," though it has a Sunday school-level religious message, it is actually charming and delightful in tone.

In those earlier days, he was also happy playing his piano. My father, who somewhat resembled Bing Crosby, and also had a nice tenor singing voice, would sit with naturally relaxed posture at his mother's black, baby grand piano, which he moved from Ohio into our small Chicago apartment. And though he could read music, he'd play without sheet music, and with flowing improvisations such glorious works as "The Holy City," or he'd *ad lib* according to his own interior music. He was quite musically gifted, and as with his poetry-writing gift, almost mysteriously so, like an idiot *savant*. He could hear a song on the radio, and though never having heard it before; he'd sit down at the piano and duplicate it perfectly.

He could play with heart-choking expressiveness. My father had a light touch, and his renderings exquisitely demonstrated the subtle musical and emotive nuances of the piece. His hands, though not large, were agile; he played arpeggios with glittering glissando performance, in any key, up and down the keyboard. "Oh pshaw, that's just runs," he'd demur to his admirers. Or if the music called for it, he could play a bluesy rhythm, or a rocking gospel music beat.

In contrast, my mother also played the piano, but she sat with a straight, stiff spine; her eyes fixed on the hymn book, she appeared to be concentrating with great effort. If she hit a wrong note, she grunted in disgust and quickly glared down at her hands, trying to find the offending finger. Most of the time she hit all the right notes, but she banged and clunked away at the piece, always sounding like a child at her lessons.

Because of his versatility, my father was sought out by singing groups as a valuable accompanist; and I remember several groups or church choirs he played with. One group was called "The Southern

115

Gospelaires," and they made several albums, one being *Wonderful Savior.*

He preached and played at Chicago rescue missions such as Pacific Garden Mission and Glad Tidings Mission, and would bring me along, sometimes Esther too, and have us get up and sing while he accompanied us on the piano. I was very uneasy at this and never liked to sing in front of this, or any audience, but Esther seemed to enjoy it.

He and I went to the bank and we bought the groceries together. In subzero temperatures, we walked to the neighborhood filling station to buy oil for the stove that heated our tiny apartment. He made me help him carry the ten-gallon drum back home; I did not have gloves and the metal handle froze my hand, anesthetizing it from the pain of the red welts made across my hand. Later, he did break down and buy a used Flexible Flyer sled, and we pulled the oil drum home on it through the snow.

But I was his reluctant companion, always wondering when he'd fly into one of his unpredictable rages. He greatly depended on me as his traveling companion and I soon realized why. I was along to take care of him when he had one of his frequent seizures. I realize now that he felt somewhat more secure when I was with him, but on the other hand, he resented being dependent on me or on anyone else. Of all people, though, it was easiest for him to be dependent on me. It would not be quite so embarrassing for him to have a seizure around me, as compared to an acquaintance. I was a very benign and non-threatening person, and he had the opportunity to feel himself superior by his constant beating up on me, whenever he was angry at the world. And I was intelligent and conscientious enough to be depended upon to do the right thing.

Of course, he was quite selective in whom he beat

up on; he would never mouth off to his boss or pick a fight with co-workers, he wasn't that stupid. He only beat up on those he didn't think could or would fight back, like me as a kid, later my mother, than later my younger brothers, his stepchildren and always their pet Beagles.

In my freshman year, Esther and I rode the Greyhound bus to Tennessee to visit our father. We stayed at his lady-friend Daisy McCallister's house. On Sunday morning before going to church, with no provocation, in his Sunday suit, white shirt and tie, he started beating me with his fists about my head and face, in front of Daisy, her two teen-aged daughters, and Esther. Daisy called the police, and they contacted the Home on our behalf. The police ordered him to leave Daisy's house immediately and to stay away from us. Later that afternoon, under police escort, we caught the next bus back to Illinois.

Why is it that in all the time I lived at the Home, I was never hit by a house parent or any other adult, but he was always beating up on me, even as a fully grown young woman?

My sister, brothers and I have talked about his selective violence. He never beat up on my sister because she was his mother's namesake and resembled her. He did try to beat up on his stepdaughter, until her mother stepped in and told him if he ever touched her again, he'd be in the most serious trouble he could imagine; and he of course never bothered her again.

My mother, in similar circumstances, should have likewise defended me, but she never did.

He made sure that I memorized all the necessary addresses and phone numbers; he knew that I could get us home safely, if needed. He taught me how to get around in Chicago with him; how to summon the police, how to fight, particularly how to kick a man in

117

the nuts as the surest offensive move, and how to hide *his* wallet in my sock whenever we went out.

Every month he got a small box in the mail. It made a mysterious and muffled rattle when I shook it. Inside were several small, variously shaped, and almost artistically constructed boxes of pills. Pill boxes were not "tamper proof," not even sealed in those days. He taught me how to count out his medicine for him. Each box contained a different pill or capsule and had a thin cotton sheet under the lid. In one box were dainty, lavender tablets, which were scored in the middle and had a bitter smell. Another box had small, smooth, white capsules, each with a red stripe around it. He was supposed to take a handful of multi-colored tablets and capsules three times a day, but many times he didn't take his medicine.

One night, coming home on the CTA bus, he had a particularly bad seizure. We were tired and had been sitting quietly, bumping along on the bus. The other passengers were similarly quiet and resigned to the bus ride, idly watching the city night lights flash by through the windows. Both of us could tell when a seizure was coming on; he looked at me with his typical prodromal expression on his face, eyes wide with terror. He gave me a look of embarrassment, as though he was trying to be nonchalant about the seizure which we both knew was whipping up its fury. At the same time, his periorbital muscles contracted, twisting his face into grotesque features. It seemed as though he was trying with all his might to keep his mouth from flying open, and as I imagined, screaming out the terror that was apparent all over his face. His efforts caused obscene-sounding lip-smacking, which as the electrical storm thundered across his brain, eventually gave way to grunting, groaning, and snorting.

I was terrified at seeing my father in such agony.

118

He seemed so utterly pitiful I could hardly stand it. Eventually his whole body was wildly convulsing until he ended up on the floor of the lurching bus. All the passengers stared at us. I did as I was taught to do: ease him down onto the floor, onto his side if possible; loosen his collar; not stick my fingers or anything else into his mouth; and probably most difficult of all—just watch him carefully so that he didn't harm himself, and wait until the thunder passed.

I could see that he'd been incontinent of bowel and bladder and had soiled his clothing. I knew that after the seizure had thrashed him he'd be incapacitated with confusion, and so I made sure that we got off the bus at the right stop. He leaned on me and stumbled like a drunk as we walked the short distance to our front door. Inside, he collapsed on the couch and slept deeply without moving until morning.

How frightened I was to see my father so weak and whipped. I knew that his epilepsy was humiliating for him. I guess he also felt guilty that his own birth caused the death of the mother he never knew.

I learned at too young an age how weak and impotent we can be under "the slings and arrows of outrageous fortune." I've been learning the thunder all my life, learning to read the thunder; but there have been so many times I've wished I didn't know anything about it at all.

***

I knew exactly how much money he made because he'd sit me down at the kitchen table on Saturday mornings with his paycheck and the bills. He would have me write down each item, as he dic-

119

tated to me. He delighted in codifying each bill according to his alpha-numeric filing code system, with which he used to organize a four-drawer, oak filing cabinet. He was always trying to appear smart and secretive; I guess he didn't think that I knew what he was referring to. Then he'd have me add everything up and compare what we owed with his net pay. He'd have me do the "casting out nines" trick that he'd taught me, to check my addition.

Most of the bills were for non-priority things, things you couldn't eat. Someone had sold him life insurance policies for all of us, which he later cashed all in anyway. He'd also been sold on new bedding because he worked as a shipping clerk at National Bedding Company at that time. We were starving but we had life insurance policies, new beds and a tape recorder.

He allotted $10.00 a week for groceries, which included formula for my infant brother Larry. Except for instant dry milk, he would not buy milk for Esther and me because it was too expensive. He and I walked the five blocks to the Jewel food store and pulled the groceries home in a cart or on the sled.

Each week he bought a box of saltine crackers, tomato soup, and a carton of Quaker oatmeal and sometimes a gallon jar of peanut butter. He made a large pot of oatmeal and put it in the refrigerator with no lid on it. He told us that this is what we were to eat for the rest of the week. I can still see that big pot of oatmeal sitting in the bottom of the refrigerator; it was the only thing there. In several days, the top became dried out and underneath, the oatmeal congealed and separated from the water. Topped with "blue milk" made from powered mix that we had to drink, that oatmeal was pretty hard to swallow no matter how hungry I was.

We visited the Olson Rug Company's Waterfalls and Rock Garden, on Diversey at Pulaski (Crawford) many times, as the property was decorated thematically, according to the seasons and holidays, and there was no admission charge. Upon returning home, we got off the Diversey Street bus at Grand Avenue.

At the corner of Grand and Pulaski there was a hotdog stand called "Jimmy's Wieners." You could get five hotdogs for $1.00 then. A couple of times, my father bought wieners here, especially when my mother begged him. He had a good appetite and liked to eat too, so he really didn't mind a good excuse to buy Jimmy's Wieners. When going to Jimmy's from our apartment, I'd walk with him the several blocks to pick up our wieners; we walked west on Grand Avenue to Pulaski and crossed the street at the busy intersection. Jimmy's Wieners was on the northwest corner of that intersection.

The place was always hustling busy and smelled like French fry heaven. I watched the Hispanic men all in white caps, tee-shirts, trousers and aprons, assemble the wieners.

They fetched the buns with metal tongs from behind a metal roll-top door; the steam billowed out when they rolled it open, then they'd quickly slam the door shut again. They laid the steaming buns into stainless steel trays with many bun-sized compartments; then they tapped the wieners into the buns with their fingertips. And then with a small spatula they slathered on mustard, then spooned on pickle relish, then piled on chopped onions and bits of tomato, and finally a couple of green hot tamales.

Then they laid each dressed dog perpendicular to the corner of a foot-square piece of white deli wrapping paper, then brought that tip just over and under the hotdog; then the two adjacent tips of the square paper were each in turn folded across the hotdog; and finally it was rolled up to meet the remaining forth corner tip of the square sheet of paper. I couldn't wait to get home to eat mine. I always picked out the tamale and gave it to my mother. When we bit into those hotdogs, the casing snapped and salty hotdog juice squirted right into our mouths. The bun was soggy soft and the mustard and relish ran down our chins, and we spilled onions and tomato bits on the table and onto our laps. We each ate one and my father ate two; it was a meal for us made in heaven and only cost $1.00 in 1960.

***

In the months just before we were placed in the Children's Home, someone gave us a small, black and white television with a "rabbit ears" antenna; this was an untold luxury to us and a glorious diversion from our grim existence. My father would occasionally buy a half gallon carton of Neapolitan ice cream. Sitting in the dark apartment late at night, he'd thoroughly enjoy himself watching boxing or wrestling while consuming the entire carton. I would creep into the room to watch the television with him and watch him eat the ice cream; and much to my surprise, he didn't holler at me, but I didn't dare ask him for any ice-cream.

We had a floor model radio; it was set in a handsome mahogany cabinet which was handcrafted like a musical instrument for a warm, resonant sound. Its large front speakers were covered with woven fabric grill cloth; it had gold tuning knobs and white keyboard-like buttons to press down. I spent hours sitting on the floor mesmerized by the evocative classical music and the imaginative stories narrated by very believable voice actors and embellished with exciting background auditory cues.

My mother tuned to Chicago radio station WMBI, which broadcasted such programs from Moody Bible Institute as "Mother Teresa's Story Hour," John Doremus's six o'clock evening program of classical music called, "Candlelight and Silver," and "Unshackled," from Pacific Garden Mission.

She also listened to the "The Breakfast Club," which curious to me, she very much enjoyed. I'd hear her laugh awkwardly and inappropriately, in annoying bursts; and she'd carry on a conversation with the program voices, which always embarrassed me even if no one else was around.

***

In my efforts to have an objective memory of my childhood, I tried for many years to recall any pleasant memories about my parents. I remembered that they each had nice singing voices and in the earliest days they occasionally sang together, while my father played the piano.

Following is a poem based on that recollection. One Sunday, I'd heard them over a loudspeaker while in a church nursery with my sister, as they sang during the Sunday morning church service. The name of the church was Elm-LaSalle Bible Church. This is my last memory of them singing together and the only pleasant memory I have of this dubious duet.

It is also my only recollection of seeing my mother in a church, though my father and I attended frequently.

Some time later, I heard her declare to him that

she was Jewish.

"What do you mean you're Jewish?" he demanded incredulously, "You can't just say you're Jewish. Jewish is a race, a culture, not just a religion. What do you mean you're a Jew?"

"You can convert," she demurred.

"Oh yeah, so who's a Jew convert that you know?"

"Marilyn Monroe and Elizabeth Taylor."

"Oh gosh," he spat out, "they're crazy women just like you."

"In the Bible, Naomi the Moabite, who wanted to go with her Jewish mother-in-law Ruth, and Abraham, the father of the Jews was from the land of Ur. Couldn't you say they were converts?"

He glared at her in disgust.

Try as I would, I couldn't sustain the pleasant memory of their singing together for any length of time, even for just the duration of the poem, and so the memory turns sadly tragic at the end.

Guardian Angel

The church nursery
down a cool flight of stairs
was a wide-open room
where colorful toys were scattered
and wooden cribs lined
gaily decorated walls.
On one such wall a picture hung:
an angel hovering gently over
a boy leading his sister
across a swinging bridge;
the planks clacking
the water swirling below.

124

The baby-sitter is soft and
smells like flowers;
she gathers and hush-holds me.
Sister Esther gently snoring
behind wooden slats,
a fan buzzing at her damp dark head.
Across the room a crackling box
with a large, warmly-lit dial;
"Listen," says the baby-sitter
nodding to the singing box.
A woman's voice, rich and warm
like roasted chestnuts
carried the melody
gilded by a clarion tenor; he
harmonized like pure gold.
I must have looked bewildered.
Yes I was proud of my parents singing
but I knew that he would beat me
and bash me again and again
and I knew that she was
safely lost to us;
could not be found
behind murky green eyes.
And yet the words of their song:
"I sing because I'm happy
I sing because I'm free
for his eye is on the sparrow
and I know he watches me."

Part Five

Ground School
(1970-1981)

11. Getting Through College

When I graduated from high school in June 1970, I already had a job at Black Dot in Crystal Lake, Illinois, as a proofreader. I immediately moved out of the Home and rented a room in a private home. I'd been accepted at Southern Illinois University, but was anxiously awaiting a letter saying I'd been awarded the Illinois State Scholarship, which would pay all of my tuition. I got that letter late, the last week in August, and had little time to make a decision and then shift gears. But I did decide to resign my job at Black Dot in order to attend SIU.

I was proud of having landed the job at Black Dot. They had provided me with extensive on-the-job training, beginning with proofreading galley sheets; and I knew even then that I was lucky to receive training for this specialized skill.

My supervisor was a mature woman with an ample figure. She had dark eyes and a reassuring smile. Her dark hair was always professionally styled, bouffant in the front with a curly bun in the back. She always wore a sweater draped over her shoulders, held in place with a gold clasp. Ms. Warner was patient with the steep sloop of my learning curve, never cross, always encouraging and good-natured. She was a working supervisor, always sitting at her desk, in a proper but relaxed posture, proofreading right along with the rest of us; although her galley sheets look considerably more complex than ours. So detail oriented was she that on our breaks, she would crochet pastel-colored angora sweaters with her large, deft hands.

Betsy was also an older woman, always sun-tanned, wearing short skirts which showed off her shapely legs, and a kicky hair-do. She was so cute and utterly charming with her frequent, hoarse giggle. Betsy told me that she had grown up in Georgia. In her cubicle, she was always snacking on salt-free Melba toast and Swiss cheese, because as she said, she had high blood pressure and had to watch her salt intake. She would pile paper-thin slices of Swiss cheese onto pieces of Melba toast and put them on my desk, without me ever asking for one. I couldn't believe that someone as wonderful as her could have high blood pressure, or any other problem.

To my surprise, they had a going-away party for me complete with several gifts of college clothes. I'd only been employed there a couple of months. My co-workers were all so friendly and encouraging; my experience at Black Dot was by far the most affirming one I'd ever had yet, and it was even "out in the real world," which I'd found to be warm and friendly at Black Dot, not cold and cruel. Because of their kindness, I certainly did have mixed feelings about leaving.

In retrospect, I'd have saved myself a lot of money if I'd stayed at Black Dot and completed my first two years at McHenry County College, both in Crystal Lake. I'd have been on a career path quite suitable to my natural abilities and in a friendly, familiar environment.

But even though I was pretty sure that I wouldn't have enough money to attend SIU for more than one semester, I wanted to get away; and SIU was as far away as possible while still in Illinois. I wanted to have at least one, even if short, experience on a large university campus. As it has turned out, that was the only semester I've ever lived on a university campus.

I went to Southern Illinois University, instead of to the University of Tennessee or any other out-of-state school so that I could use the Illinois State Scholarship for four years, which would pay all of my tuition—up to a certain amount—and that amount easily covered any Illinois public university tuition.

I simply could not have attended college without the Illinois State Scholarship.

Thank you, Illinois taxpayers.

***

Mr. Leeds drove me to Southern Illinois University-Carbondale in early September 1970. I'm sure he had doubts about the whole idea; and as my house parent, he knew that I couldn't afford to stay there for very long. But he never asked any questions about my financial plans or anything else.

As a freshman at SIU, I was not allowed to keep my car on campus and so Mr. McIntyre let me park it in his driveway, where he lived in the staff housing adjacent to the Woodstock Children's Home.

At SIU, my assigned room was on the ninth floor of Neely Hall. SIU was overwhelming and every bit as amazing as I thought it would be. Kids seemed to have an infinite supply of money, parental support, carefree time and thoughts, and self-confidence. I didn't have any of that and so found a job immediately and worked as many hours as they'd let me on the university work-study program for minimum wage.

When I left the Home, they gave me all the money I'd saved over the years. I used all that, plus the money I earned while working concurrently, to pay for one semester of room and board, dining room passes, and textbooks at SIU. The Illinois State Scholarship was to pay tuition but not room and board or anything else.

130

During Thanksgiving and Christmas vacations, all dorm residents had to evacuate the premises, taking all their belongings with them. I had no place to go and no way to get there. I stayed with classmates at their homes during vacations and bummed rides, between Woodstock and Carbondale, from the parents of my Woodstock Community High School classmates also enrolled at SIU.

When I came back to Woodstock over the Christmas holidays in 1970, the first thing I did was to go to Mr. McIntyre's driveway to get my car. There it sat in the driveway almost covered in snow. The apple green finish and the brown convertible top were scarcely visible through the snow. I dug it out and even though I'd had the foresight to leave the doors unlocked, I had to tug hard to get the frozen doors open. I got in, slammed the gas pedal down several times to choke it, depressed the frozen clutch and moved the stiff gear shift on the floor into neutral position.

Even the ignition was so frozen it was difficult to turn the key. But much to my delight, the Volkswagen fired right up on the first try. Then as it idled raggedly, I scraped layers of ice off the windshield.

I found a shovel in Mr. McIntyre's garage and shoveled out a path to the road. By that time, the engine was running smoothly and it was a few degrees warmer inside. With the windshield defroster just barely keeping a small circle of glass clear, I backed the crunching frozen tires out and drove off for a pleasure ride.

***

I knew that I had no more money to pay for room and board, not to mention my ongoing car payments, insurance and maintenance, after the first semester at SIU; and I wouldn't be able to earn enough on the work-study program to pay my way.

But since I'd been awarded the Illinois State Scholarship for four years, I was determined to find a way to take advantage of that gift. I figured if I paid for and successfully passed my first semester at SIU while holding down a job, the Home or the Evangelical Child Welfare Agency which had placed me in the Home, might help me with the room and board for future semesters.

Students could not register for subsequent semesters without paying at least a proportion of their room and board up front, and all debt from the previous semester had to be paid in full.

I could not raise the money and the Home would not help me. So, I left SIU after successfully completing the first semester and returned to Woodstock.

I finished the remainder of my first two years at McHenry County College, in Crystal Lake, Illinois, where I rented a room in the home of MCC playwright, Laurie Oldegaard. I did college work-study and other part-time jobs; and with the Illinois State Scholarship and the Illinois Guaranteed Loan, I finished my baccalaureate degree at Roosevelt University in Chicago, just four years after high school graduation.

***

While I was trying to finish up my undergraduate degree at Roosevelt University, I received a most unsettling letter from the State of Illinois,

132

Department of Mental Health. It advised me that pursuant to Chapter 91, Section 12 of the Mental Health Law, children may be liable for the medical bills and support of their biological parents.

They were threatening to force me to support my mother. As this particular State of Illinois department didn't know me from Adam's housecat, I knew it had been my mother who'd given them my name and address. I was livid at her for doing this, one of her many manipulative stunts.

She conveniently left out the fact that she and my father had given up their custody and guardianship of Esther and me, and had dumped us in the Children's Home. I thought *when can I ever escape the toxic influence of my parents? Haven't I had enough of their rejection and cruelty for a lifetime?*

Since my parents' divorce, my mother had bounced in and out of Elgin State Hospital, and every time she was released her into her own custody, but she simply could not live by herself. She lived with my sister and her husband for a while but that situation and several others that we had set up for her failed, and now she was trying to manipulate circumstances so that I would be legally forced to support her.

I knew it would be a simple matter of my clueing in the authorities, but I was furious that she was still selfishly trying to ruin my life; and I'd be damned before I'd allow her to manipulate me like this. I was having enough trouble taking care of myself, and I sure didn't need her and this nuisance to deal with. I hadn't the wherewithal or the interest to support her. I thought, *Geez, haven't I had enough of this woman's evilness? When will I ever be rid of my abusive parents?*

I called the state folks and told them the story. It was true, as I suspected, that she conveniently didn't tell the state bureaucrats the minor details of how she and her husband grossly defaulted in their parental responsibilities. They immediately agreed that under these circumstances, which my mother neglected to tell them, I was of course in no way liable for her support. But I had to provide proof—legal affidavit of my claims.

So, I called the ECFA—the Evangelical Child and Family Agency in Chicago, which had placed me in the Woodstock Children's Home in 1963 (at that time they were know as the ECWA—Evangelical Child Welfare Agency) and explained the situation to them. They readily provided me with the legal papers that I needed. I asked them to give me two sets of the legal affidavit, just in case I ever had to go through this kind of nonsense again. I forwarded one set of the papers to the friendly folks at the State of Illinois Department of Mental Health, and I never heard another word from them again.

In the course of the conversation, I told Ms. Wheeling that I was just about to complete my BS degree. She didn't say a thing about that, didn't encourage me to finish, didn't congratulate me for getting that far, and most of all, didn't offer to help.

The logistics of figuring out how to put myself through college was a bit overwhelming for me, a throwaway kid with no guidance counselor, no parents and no self-confidence. I filled out numerous financial-aid forms and applications—and every year they had to be resubmitted.

I applied and sat for the ACT and SAT exams. I interviewed with various college and financial-aid officers, and it was obvious they had little experience in dealing with a Home kid, sitting alone in their office, trying by the sheer force of her determination, to lift herself off the scrapheap of society; trying to put herself through college with no advocate, no

134

mentor, no financial support, no nothing.

I have no idea where I got the gumption to do this. I had no self-confidence, not even confidence in my intelligence. I was filled with shame and humiliation about my ward-of-the state and Home kid status, which was constantly being brought up to me and questioned by the college bureaucrats. They acted like they didn't believe it. I actually expected that at anytime I'd be told that the likes of me, a ward of the state, a throwaway kid, a burden on society, wasn't even allowed to attend college anyway.

I crawled and slunkered into the registrar and financial aid offices—who did I possibly think I was to "deserve" a college education? But this was the way I was regarded by absolutely everyone and anyone who knew that I was trying to finish college. I received no encouragement from anyone whatsoever to finish college.

On top of that, it took a huge effort to concentrate on anything, or to travel even a short distance from apartment, given my minute by minute struggle with agoraphobia.

Thinking about all these things made me weary when I was trying to get the State of Illinois and my mother off my back. I knew that I had to somehow finish my college education if I had any hope of getting a job, supporting myself, and maybe even getting my own home.

***

On March 11, 1972, in the Greeneville, Tennessee *The Sun Week-Ender,* a front page feature article of my father, Paul Webster Hall, entitled "Piano-Playing Parson and Poet" went on and on for six pages. It included eleven photos and eighteen of his reported "over 350 poems."

The front page photo was of him at the piano, with his wife, her three children and my brothers Larry and Phillip all gathered around singing. There was no mention anywhere of me and Esther in this article, and certainly his poem "Two Little Girls with Cute Little Curls" was not among the many published in this feature story.

After his father died in 1965, my father fled Illinois with "his boys" and divorced my mother. He had literally kidnapped them from their suburban Chicago foster homes and fled to Tennessee. The reason he fled was because the State of Illinois had begun to put the pressure on him to give up my younger brothers for adoption, since he couldn't take care of them, instead of letting them also waste away, in foster homes.

He had long since abandoned Esther and me, and didn't seem to care at all how long we languished in the Children's Home, but he adamently wanted to keep my younger brothers. So he fled to Tennessee and then divorced my mother from Tennessee, while she was a patient in Elgin State Hospital, Illinois.

He soon found another woman he could con into marrying him. She had three children, a job, and her own home; so he figured she could take care of him. He and my two younger brothers moved in with her and her three children, into their rural east Tennessee home. He lived there until his wife died of breast cancer in 1993. After she died, his three step-children, who despised him, threw him out of their childhood home. He went from there to government-subsidized housing and is now living in a nursing home.

After Esther had heard about this 1972 newspaper article, she and her husband drove from

Michigan and showed up at his Baptist church on a Sunday morning with her two babies, demanding to be recognized as his daughter.

I also showed up at his church alone, several years later. I'll never forget his stammering when one of the male parishioners exclaimed, "Paul, is this big kid really yours? Do you have anymore secret kids?"

12. Facing Down and Fighting Inner Demons

After I finished my B.S. degree at Roosevelt University, Chicago, in December 1974, I took a job at Motorola in Schaumburg, Illinois. As I was interested in electronics and business, and I had taken a couple of statistics courses in college, I pushed hard to sell myself to the Quality Assurance Department. I wanted to land their job advertised as Quality Assurance Statistician; and I did succeed in getting the job.

I had been fascinated with radios since my childhood days sitting on the floor listening to our floor model, vacuum tube radio; and I was interested in the business of electronic communications, which really started to take off in the early 1970's.

Soon after I got this job, I became more interested in the technical aspects of the business and completed a two-year, on-the-job, electronic technician's training course provided for me by Motorola. I was there when their first citizen's band radio, Mocat, was designed, tested, and manufactured at the Schaumburg facility. As I recall, there was one other American-made citizen's band radio on the market at the time.

I was involved with the Quality Assurance group that field tested the radio. I was given a prototype radio along with the other QA engineers, so that I could "field test" it with them on our daily commutes to the plant. The radio was assigned to be operated on a frequency entirely separate from any other radio transmitters and receivers, and our communications mainly involved noting our mobile transmitting or receiving location, the threshold for breaking squelch

139

and associated signal strength, audio quality, and so forth.

Other than that, it was just jabbering, awkward attempts at sounding intelligent over the airwaves, and mostly just fun. With today's advent of cell phones, some people believe they are the first to have thought of the notion that it is dangerous to operate two-way radios while driving, but people have been operating two-way radios and ham radios in cars for years. A cell phone is just a type of two-way radio.

In 1976, one of the section managers helped me to install the radio and the low-band antenna into my black-on-grey 1974 Dodge Charger Special Edition. The actual radio was always in the trunk; and it was only the control head that was under the dashboard.

I thoroughly enjoyed my employment at Motorola and learned everything that I could soak up. In my position at this large corporate facility, I was exposed to many aspects of the business: production, engineering, field service, quality control, marketing, cutting-edge technology, and corporate issues.

It was all exhilarating to me; and I felt fortunate to have landed a job at Motorola, because except for engineering positions, the job market was tight when I finished college in December 1974. I had several supervisors who were generous with their knowledge and experience, and were excellent mentors; but I was severely limited by my lack of advanced mathematics or an engineering degree, and I knew it. I was frustrated knowing that I could not advance in a technical career at Motorola, as I'd wanted to, without advanced formal education in math and engineering.

Coincidentally, a nearby, small manufacturer of optical equipment which did most of its business with the United States government, made me an offer of a salary and career experience that I couldn't refuse, as Manager of their Quality Control Department.

I left Motorola to take that job, but stayed with them only a short time as I just could not get interested in their business, the company, or my job. Then I took a job at Western Electric Corporation, in Rolling Meadows, just a few minutes from where I lived in Schaumburg.

Soon after taking the position at Western Electric as an Engineering Associate, I was one of nine persons selected from our four-state region to participate in a Corporate Personnel Development Plan (CPDP). This training program included attending graduate school part-time to complete a Masters' in Business Administration, which was to be paid for, in full, by Western Electric. I'd completed four courses toward an MBA degree at Roosevelt University by the time I'd decided to pursue a new life in North Carolina.

***

During all this time, I suffered from a strange and crippling anxiety which seemed to manifest itself as agoraphobia. I'd struggled with acute anxiety every day of my life from the early 1970's to 1984, just after I'd moved to North Carolina and began my gender transition. After that, the agoraphobia, and then all anxious feelings very gradually but eventually completely dissipated.

I remember when this anxiety demon first came upon me, though it was an innocent and benign occasion. I was standing in the cafeteria line at Roosevelt University. Suddenly I experienced a severe attack of vertigo; the room was not spinning, but

141

instead it was I who seemed to be pitching and lurching. I had to put down my tray and hang onto the counter—then I had to quickly get down onto the floor. I was frightened and embarrassed, though I never lost consciousness. At the time, I had no medical knowledge of vertigo or its symptoms, nor did I know anything about anxiety attacks. All I knew was that my heart was pounding wildly fast, and my legs felt so weak I couldn't stand up.

I felt confused; and a sense of fear, dread and terror gripped me. I could not figure out why I had experienced these frightening physical sensations, and that made me feel even more anxious. I was gripped with worry and fear that it, whatever it was, would happen again at the most inconvenient time such as while commuting into Chicago or driving. I could only fear the worst, though I really didn't know what that might be, but it most certainly felt as ominous as losing my mind or dying.

This state of mind soon calcified into an obsessive hypervigilance of my interior life that manifested itself as agoraphobia, though I was anxious all the time, not just outside or in the car. At the time, I did not have any understanding of my suffering, including possible medical reasons for these symptoms.

Now I remember that just prior to my first vertigo attack, I had visited the infirmary at Roosevelt University with upper respiratory symptoms. I remember having several swollen, tender, right-sided, post-auricular lymph nodes, which are still palpable to this day, although not tender.

Now I also remember being diagnosed with serous otitis media—fluid in my right middle ear, in 1971, just after returning to Woodstock from SIU. I had gone to see Dr. Johnson because I'd perceived a crepitus rattling or bubbling, in my right ear. To this day, I still have chronic right nasal congestion and

142

associated fluid accumulation in my right ear. For this reason, I frequently pinch my nostrils, close my mouth, and blow hard. This forces air up through my eustachian tube and into my middle ear, causing my ear to pop, thereby forcing accumulated fluid in the middle ear space to properly drain out, and back down the eustachian tube, to where it empties next to the adenoids at the upper throat, behind the nose.

I now believe that the vertigo attack in the Roosevelt University cafeteria line was likely a result of my having viral labyrinthitis. I also believe that because of my anxious childhood, I was generally at risk to suffer anxiety as a result of this, or any similarly frightening and bewildering experience.

Finally, the vertigo attack may have been particularly frightening to me because I subconsciously remembered my father's public seizures, his total loss of mental and physical control, and the horrified and disdainful reaction of many onlookers.

Initially I'd never heard of agoraphobia. I only knew that I was in a constant state of intense anxiety which never relented in over ten years. I did not know why this had come upon me so suddenly or what caused it. The fact that I was nearly paralyzed with agoraphobia as opposed to some other phobia further exacerbated my anxiety, because I knew that I just had to get to work to support myself.

I'd been acutely aware all my life that I had to take care of myself; there simply was no one else. I never in my life have had a safety net, and perhaps this knowledge was the source of my anxiety. How inconvenient for me to have agoraphobia. If I had to suffer a phobia, why couldn't it at least be something that likely wouldn't interfere with my ability to support myself?

If I had been able to articulate my anxiety, I would have said something like this: I was anxious because

143

I was acutely aware that I was totally alone in the world, and would likely remain so. Getting married to generate a family for myself and an illusion of security, which is what many people unwittingly do with their loneliness anxiety, was not an option for me.

Furthermore, I was greatly ashamed that I was afflicted with this thing, whatever it was, because even though no one else knew about it, I was greatly disabled by my anxiety and I was not able to reassure myself. The distance I was able to travel in my car without anxiety was nil.

However, I was able to run many carefree miles in my neighborhood. Running was the only thing I could do which did not only distract me from my anxiety, but was also mentally soothing and physically exhilarating.

In retrospect however, I did cope. I did drive myself to work, to MBA classes at RU's extension campus—then in Arlington Heights, and to every appointment that I'd committed to; but it was always with extreme anxiety. I was increasingly anxious about commuting into Chicago, even by train. But I knew that I just had to finish my education.

When I did complete my degree I was relieved beyond words, but was so ashamed of my anxiety struggles, which I knew had greatly impeded my learning, that I felt I didn't rightly deserve the degree. I didn't attend my graduation ceremony, held at Roosevelt University's historic Auditorium Theatre, on Michigan Avenue in Chicago. There was nobody to be there with me anyway.

Luckily, I was able to find my job at Motorola, just after graduating. By all outside appearances I excelled at my job and received excellent reviews, raises, and promotions. But inwardly, I knew that there was always this anxiety demon close by and I was never able to relax, not even for a moment.

I knew that most people would have been appalled if they knew the extent of my mental suffering; and so I was not able to tell any one about this. I feared they'd think I was crazy and would want to dope me up with sedatives or worse, psychotropic drugs. I was so hypervigilant that I could not have allowed myself the least bit of sedative or mind-altering substance, not even a drink. I never drank a drop of alcohol until I was thirty-six years old. I couldn't relax enough to have a drink; the relaxing effect of a drink would have been too frightening to me.

Every activity was a huge effort, even going to the grocery store, and so I avoided everything except going to work. So full of shame, I felt that I was just barely coping. The entire issue with all its shame tormented me every waking minute of every day. I was very hard on myself. I tried but just couldn't put it out of my mind. I wasn't even sure what it was that I was trying to put out of my mind. I wanted desperately to shake off the mental burden that so weighed down my spirits.

The whole enigma was so frustrating, as I mulled it over and over again, alone in my apartment, trying to figure out what was wrong with me. How could this terror, whatever it was, come upon me when I had been so sturdy, so utterly independent and alone all my life?

I had gone to church camp every year of my life as a kid, starting at age five, without knowing another child there at all. I had thoroughly enjoyed myself, socialized well with the other children and even excelled in sports, and arts & crafts. I had always been alone. *What has come over me? What's wrong with me?*

I'd known from earliest recollection that my mother was unable to take care of me; she was never there

145

for me and spent her life behind a closed door as long as I knew her.

And because of my father's severe, uncontrolled epilepsy, and because my mother was totally useless to him as well as to me, it had become my frequent responsibility to look out for him in public. I had seen the most disturbing aspects of his illness, and I had done okay with all that.

As a seventeen-year-old, I'd driven from Woodstock, Illinois, to Knoxville, Tennessee, alone in my Volkswagen. Previous to being attacked by this mysterious mental demon, I drove anywhere I wanted to without any fear at all. As a matter of fact, I loved cars and everything about cars all my life; I not only loved to drive, but excelled in driving. I had been unbelievably independent as a child and young adult; it was necessary for my survival that I was. So what was this latter-day anxiety all about? I could not figure it out, and didn't dare tell anyone about my suffering.

My father had taunted me all my life, saying in a most hateful way that I was "going to end up just like my mother." He was referring to her "nervous break-downs" and mental hospitalizations. He said this frequently to break my spirit, and at any time when he became threatened by my superior intelligence or my quiet but strong will. I can still see the hate in his eyes, which at the time terrified me because I thought that he seemed as evil as a devil trying to destroy me.

He was always ready and willing to declare that my mother was insane and that I was going to end up just like her. Now I see that this was a defense mechanism to divert attention away from his epilepsy, paranoia, disordered personality, and other problems and failures.

Certainly he knew that not too many years earlier, epileptics were believed to be possessed by the

146

devil and were thrown into the back wards of insane asylums, or worse yet, they were burned at the stake. You would think that as an ordained Christian minister, he'd have had the appropriate compassion for my mother, if he *really* thought she was mentally ill; and if he *really* was a Christian.

In a strange way, he was probably afraid of me, but I didn't realize that until many years later. I wouldn't have had the self-confidence to realize this as a child. He was afraid of me because he knew that I could see right through him. I could see right through his hateful, manipulative, evil heart. His violence was partly a cover-up for the knowledge that he was a total and hopeless failure; he had failed at everything he ever attempted. He was not even able to take care of himself, much less two wives, four children and three step-children.

I wished I'd have realized this at the time, known that I had this bit of power over him. As a defense against his fear of me, he tried every way he could to utterly destroy my spirit. I have no hesitation in saying that he tried to destroy me and would rather see me dead or locked up in the back wards of a mental institution, just as he lied and manipulated people in order to have my mother committed. He was that afraid of my intelligence, my intuition, and my silent but fierce will. But I have survived him and several other demons from hell.

And so whatever was this terrible fear that was crippling me? How ashamed I was that with all my intelligence, I could not get some understanding of this thing and "get over it." I limped through my life from that mysterious day in the cafeteria line at Roosevelt University, until just after I began my transition in 1982.

As usual, I went to the books to try to find out what was the matter with me. I learned about agoraphobia from Claire Weekes' books, but at first I was horrified and even more anxious about what I'd learned. It all sounded so clinical and psychiatrical, although I was somewhat comforted to learn that I wasn't the only person in the world who suffered this mysterious mental pain.

Claire Weekes MD spoke of "letting go," of being willing to let the fear do its worst; and she is right. Many years later, I realized that the answer at its essence really is: getting over one's fear of death, of dying alone and of losing one's personality at death. This is what we are all anxious about, and what we all must come to terms with.

I found an advertisement for an agoraphobia support group several miles away. *These people obviously didn't know what I was suffering or else they would know that people with agoraphobia just can't hop into their car and drive off to a support group; that's the whole damn problem* I thought.

Eventually, I was able to drive myself to where the support group met, and found it to be helpful, much to my surprise. I soon learned that every person there, at least to some degree, had to struggle to get to that meeting. Most of the attendees were women, but there were several men. One in particular was a psychologist, of all things. He was able to articulate to the group how his anxiety had also crippled him in his professional endeavors, but he'd obviously made great progress in dealing with his anxiety. This was helpful to me, but I still felt some alienation from the group. Even though we shared this hideous monster of crippling anxiety, I knew that I had other issues that I dare not mention to the group or to anyone else, for fear of frightening them.

I continued to limp along with this dreadful burden until one day I was so disgusted, so weary, and so broken in spirit that I knew I could not take it any

148

more. I knew that I could not live my entire life, which at that time seemed to stretch out vastly in front of me, with the mental and physical exhaustion of this anxiety. I had to break the grip of anxiety; I could not live with it any more and I was willing to do whatever necessary to be free.

I have never accepted cowardice in myself, and as soon as I ever detected it, I took any necessary measures to overcome it. I simply would never accept living with fear or cowardice especially when it impeded my pursuit of personal or professional goals. I knew that I'd reached the point that I would rather die than be afraid of this anxiety thing, whatever the hell it was that was tormenting me. I was not only going to "let go," I was going to confront.

I thought about how I could confront my fear. How could I confront something that I couldn't identify? I thought to visualize the anxiety as the ugliest, vilest demon that I could conjure up in my imagination. I imagined that my demon was determined to destroy me. Then when I had a good image of this monster, I went out to my car.

It was about 10:00 p.m. on a clear, cold night. My heart was pounding and I was trembling with the "fight or flight" adrenaline. I had chosen to fight or die, and I meant it. I got in the car, backed it slowly out of my driveway, and started slowly down the empty street. I looked all around, scanning left and right, taking in the sights of the neighborhood as if I'd never been there before.

I yelled out, my breath vapors on the air, "Okay, you fucker, come and get me." I imagined a dark creature with hideous mocking eyes. He seemed to be on the floor of the passenger's seat; but it was so dark maybe he'd come at me from behind. Whatever, it was "do or die," as far as I was concerned. I'd had enough.

I was yelling at the top of my lungs, "Come on, you fucking coward—just come on." I was so angry that I was nearly frothing at the mouth. He came at me from over my right shoulder. I grabbed the demon by his skinny, slimy neck and stared into his heathen eyes while I fought and twisted his neck with all my might. I was hollering every curse I could think of. Inside the cozy cockpit of my car, my voice was thundering loud, even to me, and the windshield was fogging up. He was snorting and spitting until I saw his bulging bloodshot eyes go lifeless and I felt his disgusting neck go limp.

I rode around for a few more minutes noticing how the stars were shimmering diamonds in the black sky. I looked widely around, again and again, noticing my surroundings as I'd never noticed them before, and as if to dare any other demon to come at me. I flicked on the car radio and enjoyed the music, something I would have previously been too hypervigilant to do. I pulled back into the peaceful cul-de-sac and into my garage. I sat for a while after turning off the engine, listening to the quiet. I got out and stood looking out at the empty streets from my open garage door. How peaceful everything was; and how harmonized and at one I felt with that peace. Then I flung down the garage door and went inside.

I slept peacefully that night; I'd made a quantum leap of progress in my inner work, in the healing of my psyche. I certainly would not have made any progress in overcoming my demons of anxiety if I'd been doped up on tranquilizers and thereby unable to even perceive my demons. Facing down inner demons has for me always been a necessary inner work that must be done in order to grow.

Part Six

Move to North Carolina and Gender Odyssey (1981-1991)

13. Forging a New Path in a Dark Wood

> In the middle of the journey of our life I came to myself in a dark wood where the straight way was lost.
>
> Ah! How hard a thing it is to tell what a wild, and rough, and stubborn wood this was, which in my thought renews the fear!
>
> Dante Alighieri, *The Divine Comedy*
> "Inferno," Canto I

I had visited the east Tennessee and North Carolina region several times in my early teens and twenties; and I fell in love with the natural beauty of the area, particularly the mountains, and decided that some day I'd find a way to move to this area of the country.

In just five years, I'd done well in my career in the electronic communications industry and at the time I decided to move, I was employed by Western Electric as an Engineering Associate. Having been selected for a management training program there, I'd just successfully completed my fourth course toward an MBA degree at Chicago's Roosevelt University graduate school; the tuition was paid for by Western Electric. Not too bad considering the acute, existential anxiety I suffered, which had mostly manifested itself as agoraphobia, making it difficult for me to drive myself to classes and to concentrate on the lectures and reading.

But I felt I was just limping along in Northern Illinois, and I longed to be in the mountains of Tennessee or North Carolina; most of all, I had a girlfriend in Charlotte, NC. So, I requested a transfer to

Western Electric's largest manufacturing facility in Winston-Salem, North Carolina. They flew me down for an interview, and on the same trip my girlfriend and I had a whirlwind of a good time. But at the same time, the government's divestiture of Ma Bell was gaining momentum. Soon the engineering and manufacturing branch of the Ma Bell monopoly, Western Electric, and the independent Bell telephone companies were to be divested; and Ma Bell was eventually split up. Nevertheless, I knew I was going to move south. I was totally alone in suburban Chicago and I wanted to move to North Carolina and begin a new life, with or without a job at Western Electric. I figured that soon there would be no Western Electric and so I resigned and moved to North Carolina on July 15, 1981. The Western Electric facility in Winston-Salem in fact ceased operations in early spring of 1983 and more than 10,000 people lost their jobs. I had already gladly given mine up for a new life.

Before I left Illinois, however, I wanted to do something entirely different; I wanted to take a fling at working at an airport. And so I took a job in the business office at a general aviation FBO (Fixed Base Operator), at Palwaukee Airport. I did this for a couple of months, and then I was ready to move south.

I did not know at the time how it would happen, but I would somehow find a way to live comfortably in my body and in my mind. As I became more willing to be who I was, my anxiety began to subside. I drove a 23-foot-long, yellow moving truck with my 1974 Dodge Charger SE in tow, from Chicago to North Carolina and had no problems with agoraphobia or any anything else, thankfully.

What a tremendous feeling to drive my big rig into the Queen City with its broad streets, grassy medians and avenues densely lined with many dogwood trees and brilliant pink and crimson azalea bushes.

I immediately got a job as the Flight Desk Manager at an area FBO (Fixed Base Operator), passed my Private Pilot's written test and continued my flying lessons. Unfortunately, the owner of the FBO, while he was piloting a Cessna 210, crashed on takeoff to Hilton Head, killing himself and a customer. The business floundered terribly and went under after a short time. What a tragic ending to a relaxing interlude in my life.

***

Then I had an urgent sense of needing to get serious, not only with my career but with my inner life.

I hired a private psychologist to administer the WAIS (Wechsler Adult Intelligence Scale) and other psychological tests to me. To my delight, I did well and the psychologist submitted my scores to American Mensa, an international high IQ society which was founded in England in 1946 by Roland Berrill, a barrister, and Dr. Lance Ware, a scientist and lawyer. The only requirement for membership in Mensa is to score within the top 2% on a standardized IQ test.

The word *mensa* means table in Latin. This image is to suggest a round-table society wherein race, color, creed, national origin, age, sexual orientation, gender status, political persuasion, educational level, or social position, do not define one's identity or status within the society.

I was pleased to be accepted as a member in April 1983, but it was also a sobering experience. It was the encouragement I needed, and it motivated to make use of my intellectual gifts. But I was thirty-one years old at the time and weary thinking about all the catching up I had yet to do, not only with my career but also with my inner work.

***

I knew that I had a superior IQ which had been documented at least twice before. The first time was in the third grade, at D.R Cameron School. The second time was when I was in the eighth grade at the Children's Home.

I, along with all the other Home kids, was sent to a mental health facility for testing and psychological evaluation. The male psychiatrist who "analyzed" me seemed so utterly stereotypical with his grey hair and beard, peering at me over silver, thin-framed reading glasses. He asked me mostly sexual questions, such as if I'd ever been sexually abused by my father or any other adult. All his questions were predicable, and he accepted my curt answers without much probing. I don't think I said more than a few words during the entire interview. It was nonsense to me; I wouldn't have told him anything, and I thought they were stupid to actually believe I would.

But out of this battery of testing, my superior IQ was again demonstrated. This testing was corroborated by achievement testing at Olson Junior High school. In every subject, including math, I was performing two and three grade levels above my eighth grade level. Mr. Waymire, a serious, nice-looking young social worker at the Home, called me into his office. He told me matter-of-factly that my IQ testing scores were superior and engaged me in the familiar conversation of double promotion. This "superior IQ talk" always mildly surprised me, because I exerted no effort in school and did only the minimum required homework. I worked odd jobs as much as I could, every evening after school and on at least one day of the weekend. I was on the Sunset Manor payroll by the time I was fifteen. Therefore I thought very little about my studies—but a lot about learning.

I was not encouraged by anyone from the Home, or the schools, toward scholastic achievement, but I was very much encouraged to be employed. This was most certainly so that I could benefit the Home by my conscientious labor, and also so that I could pay for all of my personal needs, which I did.

Mr. Waymire told me that my test scores in all subjects indicated that I could easily be double promoted. At the time, I was in the eighth grade and so this meant going from the eighth grade to sophomore year in high school. This seemed to me a daunting social challenge, and I knew I couldn't count on any adult support in this endeavor. It seemed like throwing me to the wolves, even more than I already had been.

I had zero self-confidence because of my being a ward of the state and consigned to live at the Children's Home, and I carefully tried to conceal this fact at school. The easiest way to do that was simply to avoid everyone. Interestingly, I was treated with respect by my peers; it was me who held back, mostly out of shame, avoiding friendships with others.

In retrospect, I now realize there were other reasons why I kept to myself. In my records and files, which I received from the Homes over thirty years later, several house parents and social workers noted that I was "very picky about my friends, preferring to be with older teenagers and adults; and preferring to be alone reading or working on a project." This was all quite true and I now understand that there were several reasons why I was perceived as being aloof and self-reliant.

Mr. Waymire understood my concerns, and even though the Home was motivated to move me along and out, he agreed with my decision to decline double promotion.

Even with this level of documentation of my intellectual potential, no college preparatory counseling, mentoring, or support of any kind was offered to me from the Home or the Evangelical Child and Family Agency which had placed me there. In retrospect, I certainly needed guidance, but I was not expected to succeed.

If a child, and to some extent an adult, doesn't have the necessary support and encouragement to spread their wings of potential, they likely won't have the wherewithal to find that within themselves.

I look at young people today and in particular at my wife's children who both have above average intelligence, who have had the most emotionally and financially supportive childhood one could imagine, and who are supremely self-confident. Even so, I am certain that they would not have been able to put themselves through college alone, neither financially nor emotionally, and their mother agrees with me.

A child urgently needs the emotional support and mentoring of an adult, or surrogate adult who is specifically "assigned" to him. There is nothing more unwanted than a child abandoned by his parents. Such a child is twice abandoned; by his parents and then by society. A child abandoned by his parents is "damaged goods." People rarely want someone else's damaged goods, especially discarded children.

***

157

Being accepted as a member of Mensa was a watershed in my life. I knew that being a member of Mensa was no guarantee of anything and could actually work against me. In most instances I kept my membership a secret, just as I had hid my intelligence all my life. But acceptance by Mensa was one of those serendipitous nudges of fate which not only greatly encouraged me, but soberly compelled me to be a good steward of my gifts.

I needed to be a card-carrying, *bona fide,* potentially smart person. I needed that one affirmation in my life. Though I was proud that I was a survivor, I had no self-confidence, and at that time I was somewhat beaten down in spirit and overwhelmed by all the work I still needed to accomplish. Certainly I would have never continued to push past my personal and career boundaries, some self-imposed. I would have never considered medical training if I hadn't had this secret Mensa membership card to carry in my wallet.

I have since been accepted for membership in Colloquy; an on-line high IQ society which has as its only requirement for membership to score within the top 1/2 percent on a standardized IQ test.

***

Ah, but now what to do; and in what order? Gender identity issues were now bearing down on me, and seemed to press prominence on the frontline of my psyche without conscious decision. I needed to deal with my gender conflict, which was yet another issue that was holding me back from achieving my full potential, and the shame of which was causing me to hide my light.

Since my teens, I had become increasingly with-drawn and not likely to pursue any intellectual or sports endeavors which would draw attention to me, not only in terms of my gender identity, but also possibly my inferior childhood. I had done well, appearing as an unambiguous female, in my career so far, but that was accomplished at the expense of much self-denial. I was losing the will to keep up pretenses and losing interest in living a lie just to please others. I wasn't even sure which others could possibly be worth worrying about pleasing, at such a high personal expense.

There were many disadvantages of my not having parents, such as the paucity of personal and casual support relationships, which I avoided in an attempt to avoid shame. My major disadvantage and vulnerability was not having family or surrogate family support, and my resultant feeling of being totally alone in this world, of feeling existentially alone, as I had felt since childhood.

However, in the context of considering seeking medical and surgical assistance to transform my body to match my psyche and the social ramifications of that, my dearth of family was an advantage in a way. At least I wouldn't have to worry about "what my parents would think"; and I was not married and didn't have any children. I didn't have any of the usual support relationships, but on the other hand, I wouldn't have to worry about "what people would think." It seemed to me that I certainly had paid a nice price to pursue my life in any way I chose.

My attitude soon became that I didn't give a damn what anyone might think. Where had the critics been all my life, when I was struggling to get through every single day?   To think that someone might imagine that they had a right to have an opinion about what I do with my life and my body, especially when it was to improve my ability to function in society (heaven forbid that I should ever be a burden on society) and when I was paying for all my medical and surgical treatments myself. Who could possibly have a right to voice an opinion about what I do, and pay to do, with my body and my life?

This line of reasoning propelled me towards considering gender-affirming surgeries and medical treatment. The main thing I was concerned about was to protect my employment and my employability. There was no one to take care of me except myself, as had always been so, much less to support me financially, even through my gender transition.

***

Song of the Prisoner of Chillon

I have lost my voice and
I hear the doves crying
like grey winds moaning,
but there is no
vibrato left in me.
My vocal folds flap
and are full of holes,
and my breath is so spent
like free breezes through
Byron's prisoners' rags.

If I could leave, perhaps
I'd support my spirit
with a strong diaphragm,
guide it through golden gates
of song, make a fuzzy feeling
in my chest, a resonant buzzing
in my head. What then if my voice
should return, unshackled, unfettered
through a clarion throat trilling?
What if I should then prefer
this silent song of despair?

14. Freedom Flight

In Ovid's *Metamorphoses,* the elder warrior Nestor tells the younger Achilles and his comrades the story of an invulnerable warrior of his youth named Caeneus, who had killed many men in battle against the Trojans.

One of them was the boastful Latreus, who was fierce and "bulked enormous"; he taunted Caeneus about his previous female gender. In battle, he flung a spear into Caeneus, "But the pike jumped back, the way a hailstone bounces / From a tin roof, or a pebble from a drum."

Latreus then believing his point to be dull, thought to wield the blade instead and aimed for Caeneus's loins. But the blow was deflected from Caeneus's flesh, "Clanging as if from marble, and the blade / Was shattered, and there stood Caeneus, unharmed, . . ."

Caeneus gave his enemies time to look in astonishment and wonder; then he struck Latreus, thrusting his sword to the hilt, twisting it, "and turned the weapon in his vitals, / Wound within wound."

Caeneus lived on Mount Othys and was "famous / For all he did, but the strange thing about it / Is, he was born a woman," said Nestor.

"All who listened
Clamored to hear the story, and Achilles
Was urgent: 'Tell us father: you are wise
And eloquent; we all want to hear about him.
Who was this Caeneus? Why changed, who
fought him?
Who beat him if ever beaten: where,
In what campaign did you know him?' "

In his female persona, and so named Caenis, she was famous for her beauty. Many suitors were interested, but she refused them all and wouldn't consent to any marriage. She liked to walk the lonely shore, and "Neptune got hold of her one day, / Took her by force," and afterwards he was so delighted that he promised her anything that she wanted. "Ask me for anything, / And you shall have it. What do you want the most?"

She asked to be turned into a man, so that she "may never / Again be able to suffer so." Neptune immediately granted her wish, and even as she spoke her request, her voice began to deepen. The ocean god had given his word and he kept it.

Additionally Neptune added to his promise that no man would ever again hurt Caenis: "That she should never fall by any thrust," and so Caeneus "went on his way, rejoicing / And spent the years in male pursuits, and traveled / All over Thessaly."

When he died, Caeneus became a great golden bird and "his wings whirred with a mighty sound." The people stood watching him circle the camp in an easy flight, his golden feathers glinting in the sun; they cheered him saying, "Hail and farewell, great Caeneus, mighty hero, flier without a peer. . . ."

***

Freedom Flight

The Phoenix is a mythical Egyptian bird, which
after living for five or six centuries in the desert,
consumed itself in fire and then rose from its ashes
to form a new life.

In the photo
she is left-side pilot,
squinting up at the compass
talking into the mike
cupped in her hand.
Earlier she'd climbed
atop each wing
lifted off the gas caps
and peered into the
iridescent, rainbow-colored
greasy-smelling fuel tanks.
Several times she'd circled the plane
inspected each item and
checked it off the pre-flight list.
In the cockpit
she'd stood on the brakes
and run up
the engine to its max
causing the plane to quiver
like a dead butterfly
on a moving windshield.
She is pretty and poised
but her heart is pounding.
She is about to take
her first solo flight.
She is learning to fly
to overcome
her fear of flying
her agoraphobia
her fear of everything.

She will steadily shove
the throttle into the firewall
and the plane will skip
down the runway,
leap into the air
wings up-stretched
embracing the wind.
The plane will feel lightweight
and different somehow,
the instructor's right-side
seat so empty.
She will climb
to traffic pattern altitude
then throttle back, level off
to straight and level flight.
And from her cozy cockpit
she will look out over her shoulder
and see the highway to the airport
the one she hadn't been able to travel
the road between the airport and her house
the house in which she had been trapped.
She will turn final,
approach the runway and
lower flaps; center the nose
scan the wingtips and
note the relative position of
the seat of her pants.
Then throttling back more
she'll aim the plane onto
the first third of the runway
careful to miss trees and
power lines on the way down.
Slower airspeed now;
the controls feel mushy in her hands.
Things busy in the cockpit:
a symphony, crashing cymbals,
blasting trumpets and banging drums.

166

Flaps all down
throttle all back
propeller fly-wheeling; and
on the ground with a screech!
Landings equal take-offs and
a new pilot guides her plane
back to the hanger.
I search the photo now
for any foreshadowing
of my other flight.
I only recognize that
she had more courage
than I'll ever have now.
And generations hence
might understand I
love her, I'm proud of her.
She kissed the face of God
and turned into her prince.

***

Simon Peter said to them, "Let Mary leave us, for women are not worthy of life."

Jesus said, "I myself shall lead her in order to make her male, so that she too may become a living spirit resembling you males. For every woman who will make herself male will enter the kingdom of heaven."

The Gospel of Thomas 114
The Nag Hammadi Library

***

Many gender transition stories begin something like this: "Ever since I was five years old, (five is always the magic age) I knew that I was born into the wrong body . . ."

Though I was particularly introspective in my youth, intuitive, keenly observant and intelligent, I wasn't so sure of any such thing. Actually, all I knew in my youth was that I was hungry. Even if I hadn't had the "poverty and parental cruelty," issues which absorbed all my energies, I doubt that I'd have been so enlightened, so young, regards my gender issues.

I knew that I was very different somehow, and I vaguely knew that something wasn't quite at peace in my innermost essence; but I couldn't have been more specific than that, especially at five years old. I could not have articulated such a thing, even though I excelled in the verbal skills.

Perhaps though, this vague knowing was at the basis of at least some of the anxiety I experienced as a youth and on into my thirties. Because as I began to accept myself and move in the direction of living as the male I am, the anxieties slowly dissipated, like a great and once immobilizing snowstorm gradually melts.

I believe that the existential loneliness and the associated anxieties of my childhood were so immediate that they obscured my gender issues until later. When the immobilizing fog of my childhood began to blow on by, I could faintly see home in the distance and was then able to travel toward what I could glimpse.

First I had to work through the anxiety of knowing that both my parents were unable even to care for themselves, much less for me. Furthermore, together they overtly sought to hold me back, repeatedly break my spirit, to do me harm, and even to kill me. I was intensely ashamed of all this, as though it was somehow my fault; and it was difficult to accept my history, but when I did, I was finally able to consider my gender issues and move on from there.

For those fortunate enough not to have any knowledge of these things, there is nothing more difficult to accept than that one's parents abused, rejected, and then abandoned him. Children want desparately to know that their parents love them and want the best for them. Children will go to great lengths to overlook abuses and crimes committed against them by their parents.

Even after I accepted my history and memories, I could not understand why my parents hadn't wanted me. I was robustly healthy, sincere, conscientious, intelligent, pleasant in demeanor; and not at all a troublemaker.

It has always been an agony for me to entertain others' insensitive questions, as to why my parents abandoned me, to which I've been subjected all my life. I have asked myself that same question a million times: *Why didn't they want me, why, why, why?* As

I get older, I actually understand it less, but am more able to realize that it had nothing to do with me.

I consider my wife's children, her grandchildren, and other well-meaning parents; and on the basis of those experiences, I can't imagine why a sane parent wouldn't want the best for their child. It seems to me that this is instinctual.

I have heard people rant about "behaviors against nature." To me, the most "against-nature behavior" is to neglect, abuse, abandon, or kill a child, especially one's own child.

***

I never despised my body, and I never would have done harm to my body. As a rule I've never been reckless with my health; although I did have a regular smoking habit as a youth, I never drank alcohol until I was thirty-six years old. I have always been conservative about accepting medical treatments and about what chemicals I would allow in my body. I can easily count on no more than three fingers the occasions that I've taken antibiotics; and to this day I've never taken any prescription drugs except testosterone.

Before my gender-affirming surgeries, I'd only been a hospital patient once as a child, and I believe the doctor admitted me chiefly because my parents weren't taking care of me. It was with this level of caution and attentiveness to my health that I approached medical and surgical assistance to achieving the fullness of my transition.

I remember the evening before my first surgery. I stood naked in front of the mirror and peered at my ambiguous body; this was difficult for me to do. But then I blessed my body saying a litany of blessings, covering all parts. I said *I bless my body; you are wondrously made by God. You've been and still are a good body, serving me well every second of every day for all these many years, even when I'm unconscious. I am so fortunate to have the gift of good health; there are no derangements of my physiological systems; for that I am grateful every day.*

I went on visualizing my heart, lungs, kidneys, and so forth, and I blessed every part of my body and gave thanks to God for it. I called forth the spirit of love and said that I loved and respected my body. Then I said, *but I'm going to have you, my body, modified slightly, so that I will be able to live comfortably inside the home of my body, and in society. I am going to slough off some parts that offend me and are not physiologically necessary to me. But I will not allow any harm to come to my body or my health.* I fell asleep imagining each part of my body, placing my hand upon it, then sending forth love and blessings to my body.

I have never despised my body, for such is an unhealthy attitude. Mine is a good body and continues to serve me well.

***

I didn't personally know anyone who'd undergone a contra-sex transition. But I recalled the story of Christine Jorgensen and that familiar media photo of her as a tall, attractive and feminine woman deplaning upon return from Denmark following her sexual reassignment surgery in 1952, the same year I was born.

I also recalled the story of Renee' Richards and

her story titled *Second Serve,* a most clever title for her story, and the literary and artistic style of Jan Morris's *Conundrum.* But I certainly didn't know of any genetic female transitioning to male.

However "When the student is ready the teacher will come," and in early 1982 while languishing in my apartment having severely broken my leg, I happened to see the Vittitow twins and their accompanying psychologist on the Phil Donahue television show. Identical twins, they both had changed from female to male gender. They presented themselves well, and I'd never before heard of the possibility of medical/surgical help in transitioning from female to male.

I experienced a knock-down jolt of recognition. From that show, I was referred to the Janus Foundation (now defunct) and from them I received several informational pamphlets and the names of a psychologist and an internist in my area; both were listed as "treating patients with gender identity dysphoria."

The next thing I did was go to a barber and had my long hair cut off short. I'd had long, thick, wavy, blonde hair for as long as I could remember, though usually wore it tied back. I don't mind saying that it was beautiful hair and I was used to heads turning wherever I went. My female beauty was a huge problem, as it would be for any person with a male psyche, who wanted society to regard him as such.

Curiously, cutting off my hair turned out to be a hugely cathartic and apparently symbolic act for me; afterwards my male psyche immediately flooded to the fore. There was absolutely no turning back. I felt, and allowed myself to feel the man that I was, and am. It was the easiest and most natural development of any in my life. I didn't have to consider what I looked like, how I preferred to dress, what was my

172

style, what was my deportment, what were my preferences, as a male. All those things and more were now naturally apparent to me. I spent no time nor wasted any psychic energy in figuring out who I was in my male persona.

Cutting off my hair was almost a more cathartic and symbolic act than my surgeries. After I allowed my male psyche to come forth, which the hair cutting surprisingly did, the subsequent surgeries were superfluous compared to the inner transformation that had already occurred. After this, things began to happen very rapidly and in most respects quite easily.

15. Self Made Man

What a piece of work is a man! How noble in reason, how infinite in faculties, in form and moving how express and admirable, in action how like an angel, in apprehension how like a god! The beauty of the world, the paragon of animals!

Shakespeare, *Hamlet*, 2.2

Consider the social ramifications for me of going, nearly overnight, from a perceived thirty-year-old female to a prepubescent male. And let me tell you, there are definitely social ramifications. The woman is treated with a lot more respect than the young male, in my experience. As a rule, females in our society are protected, and many even indulged; they are the first off the Titanic. Women are not expected to sacrifice their lives in war or in rescuing others from burning buildings.

Many will say that males are socialized to protect women. Many will say that in addition to the socially prescribed role as protector, men are biologically hard-wired and equipped to be protectors. Unless overtly threatening, females are just not roughed up by the police. Females are never reflexively perceived to be dangerous, violent or evil, and are generally believed to be of a gentle and innocent spirit. Erroneously, females are thought to possess a greater capacity for compassion and intuition, and to possess superior wisdom.

Many a young man is treated with zero respect, especially a nice-looking one, or one who shows the least bit of self-confidence. Many people will think that such a man is cocky, and needs "to be taken down a notch." By such people, he may be regarded as a despicable smartass, a testosterone-toxic, breeder-male—as one having absolutely no refinement or sensibilities whatsoever.

Men's lives had always seemed more dangerous to me, and I saw men's lives to be disposable. Young men, at least in my youth and earlier, were nothing more valuable than cannon fodder. Their lives existed to be consumed by supporting and saving others.

American men have shorter life spans by seven years on average, even if they manage to avoid being killed in a war, be assassinated or otherwise murdered in the streets. I vividly recall seeing scores of seventeen year old drafted men, a couple of years ahead of me in high school, corralled at the Chicago & Northwestern train station in Woodstock, waiting for the train to take them down to the induction center in Chicago. Many of them did not return home.

During the Vietnam War, a staggering 2.2 million American men were drafted, before Defense Secretary Melvin Laird announced the end of the draft in January 1973.

In one other example, during the four years of the Civil War, 620,000 American soldiers died on United States soil. Men's lives seemed disposable and dangerous indeed.

Society's attitude toward black men seemed even worse. In many cases black men, especially young black men, are reflexively regarded with suspicion and distrust. Many people project their racial fears and anxieties onto every black man who walks toward them down the street. I have sympathy for the young black man, who while trying to make something out of his life, has to machete his way through such prejudice and ignorance. Imagine him even trying to be magnanimous under such circumstances, trying to maintain a noble spirit, much less just "making it" in life. Because of this insight, I try to be generous in spirit toward my black brothers, whenever I can.

In view of society's generally negative attitude toward young black men, I imagine that a black female to male transsexual is in for a real eye opener of an adjustment. Men don't have careers in most cases, they have just regular jobs. They pick up your garbage, change the brakes on your car, work on the roads, build skyscrapers and bridges, repair your coronary arteries, hammer a new roof onto your house, run into blazing buildings to carry out the injured and the dead, fight wars in order to defend our freedoms—jobs that are every bit as "dirty" and underappreciated as changing a diaper, not to mention dangerous.

Of course I speak in generalities and fortunately I see some evidence that these attitudes are improving.

***

I immediately made an appointment with the referred psychologist. He was an utterly proper, polite, professional, restrained and wool-tweed sort of guy. He was so dry in his manner that our first greeting and handshake was like opening the door of a blast furnace—it took me aback.

After just a few minutes of talking to him, it became wondrously apparent that he thought I was a man wanting to transition to a female, instead of vice-versa. I let him go on for a while as I thought, *geez, this is turning out to be a helluva of a day.*

I went to his office well dressed, in unambiguously men's clothing: a dark suit, long-sleeved white shirt, conservative dark tie, men's black shoes, and

177

of course my male haircut. It seems ridiculous to me now to specify this, but the point is that I did not go to my first appointment with a gender specialist asking for his permission to be who I was, and was already living as.

I wanted to make it quite apparent that I already knew who I was and was there to solicit his support and help in achieving the fullness of my transition. I was not there to audition or beg for his approval and permission. That has always been my attitude, and it has served me well in my subsequent dealings with physicians and other professionals. This attitude came from within me, and independent of any other persons or support. I knew no other transsexuals; there was no such thing as support groups or the internet (for me) in those days. I was entirely alone in my transition. Furthermore none of my physicians or surgeons had any previous experience in providing healthcare for a female to male transsexual.

***

A Little Dab Will Do Ya

As you might imagine, I was without any concern that the psychologist wouldn't endorse medical and surgical assistance toward my gender transition since he already perceived me as a man. During our first visit, he indicated his willingness to refer me to an internist for testosterone hormone replacement therapy and I immediately made an appointment with the physician he recommended.

Dr. Cranmer spent a lot of time with me taking a history and physical. He was strictly professional, matter-of-fact, not overly warm or personable, probably as a defensive measure. But as a fiercely independent, private sort of a guy myself, that was quite okay with me. Just as with the psychologist, Dr. Cranmer seemed to accept and regard me as fully male. He prescribed testosterone at my first office visit; I was thirty years old. The effects were immediate, thrilling, and dramatic.

How can I describe the effects of a second, transsexual puberty at age thirty? It's hard enough to describe same bio sex puberty. What a remarkable perspective to have at age thirty, and even more difficult to articulate!

Things were already going fast and the effects of testosterone accelerated the transition. My voice deepened immediately and soon enough I grew a beard, which I've kept ever since. Every square inch of my body was affected; just as with any other man. My body became more lean and muscular, my hips and upper thighs narrowed, the yoke of my shirts pulled wondrously across my shoulders, and I went from a dress shirt size 15 to 15 1/2. Recently, my collars have again become too tight, necessitating having the top button moved over on all my dress shirts.

***

Running is a metaphor of life for me. And I had remembered the therapeutic benefit of running, back in my anxious days of agoraphobia. I started walking on a nearby school track to rehabilitate myself after my broken leg healed, and then soon took off running again. Since that time in 1982, I haven't missed more than a week of running and presently I run six to thirteen miles, twice to thrice per week, time permitting. I've run the half marathon several times; I am

179

not at all fast, but my life has been more about endurance, not speed. In my youth, I was better at sprinting and shorter runs. I also did well at softball, swimming, soccer, skating, acrobatics and dancing.

The most remarkable physical change, I think, has been my face. As the years pass, my face continues to get leaner, and more angular. My cheekbones, jaw and chin are prominent and masculine; and I wear a closely shaven beard, and my hair short, to accentuate this. I've grown in respectable brow ridges, which do indeed deflect the copious brow sweat I work up while running, down along the side of my face, instead of into my eyes.

I should say that the playing out of the hand of testosterone, no matter how well you play it, will not give you characteristics that genetics hasn't dealt you. You can take tons of testosterone, but if your genetics has dealt you a slight build or a lyrical voice, there will be a limit to how much you can bulk up or sing *basso profundo*.

Overdosing on testosterone may cause you to paw the ground, grow horns, and howl at the moon, but you will never look like Arnold Schwarzenegger if it isn't in your genes. And bio men who produce endogenous testosterone can develop serious side effects, such as atrophy of their testicles and the cessation of endogenous testosterone production, if they abuse exogenous testosterone.

16. The Language of God

Mathematics is the language by which God has written the universe.

Galileo Galilei

I cannot recall for sure my first fascination with numbers. Perhaps it was in the first or second grade when I learned the "casting out nines" trick, taught to me by my father as a method to check an addition problem having many addends with many decimal places. I remember my excitement and curiosity: *How clever! How does it work?* I had a sense that mathematics was inherently logical and consistent, and that there was much more to math than what I knew about.

Just after beginning my transition, I dared to enroll in math classes at Central Piedmont Community College, in Charlotte, North Carolina. I had no confidence in my math abilities, but I wanted just one chance to take a look at math and why it had stirred so much curiosity and excitement in me.

After my first algebra class, my instructor asked me to be his assistant; I worked with him in his office grading students' papers, and so I hung out daily with math instructors. How thrilling to follow and be able to understand the step-by-step derivation of the quadratic equation. I found math to be every bit as exciting as I'd remembered from my childhood. I got good grades but I worked hard to get them.

I remember when in my first quarter calculus class it dawned on me, independent of anything that the teacher said, that the first derivative of the formula for the area of a circle was (the formula for) the circumference of a circle; and that the first derivative

181

of the formula for the volume of a sphere is (the formula for) the surface area of a sphere, and so forth. *Wow! This was the most exciting stuff I'd ever heard of! This stuff actually means something; it actually refers to something in the real world; it's not just a bunch of arbitrary rules.*

I felt that I'd been given a glimpse of the most arcane secrets of the universe and I felt lucky to have some understanding of it all. This was a very heady experience for a throwaway kid like me, who figured people would wonder who I thought I was, taking up such elite studies meant only for a chosen few.

Studying math just blew my mind wide open, not only intellectually, but also in a personal sense. I became even more interested in what was going on in the world beyond me than my inner life.

As a teacher's assistant at Central Piedmont Community College, I got the idea for a course called "Math Anxiety Reduction." I was encouraged to write up a proposal and present it to the curriculum committee. I did that, and my course was accepted in the Advancement Studies Division. How proud I was to see it among the course listings in the college catalogue.

I wrote the course syllabus and objectives, and then I was invited to teach the course. In addition to the Math Anxiety Reduction course, I also taught a Developmental Algebra class. Even though I no advanced education in mathematics, I had thoroughly mastered up to the level which I had achieved. I really understood the concepts of algebra, and had not just memorized formulas.

My intent was not only to teach algebra, but to encourage other students who, like me, had no confidence in their math abilities or in much of anything else. Like me, these students were concerned that their weak math skills would impede their attaining of their educational and professional goals.

It was a rewarding experience, and I know that I helped many students. For my work in math anxiety reduction, I was nominated two different times for the CPCC "Innovator of The Year Award." The first time I lost to the retiring first and only (at that time) president of the college, Dr. Hagemeyer. The second time I lost to a team collaboration, which was headed by my Division Chief, Claude Williams.

***

I do not know what I may appear to the world, but to myself I seem to have been only like a boy playing on the seashore, and diverting myself in now and then finding a smoother pebble or a prettier shell than ordinary, whilst the great ocean of truth lay all undiscovered before me.

Isaac Newton

I was lucky to have had this learning and employment experience and I wrung every opportunity out of it that I could, but I was totally limited by my lack of a graduate degree. During the time I was employed at Central Piedmont Community College, I was in the process of trying to get my new legal name on my college transcripts, and I wouldn't have been able to prove my credentials, in my male identification, if asked. I was employed in this teaching capacity longer than I ever thought possible without proving that I had an undergraduate degree.

I hired an attorney to take care of my legal name change, which was easy enough. He also got me a new birth registration card which indicated my new name and male gender. But I subsequently had difficulty in getting Roosevelt University to accept my name change. Specifically, I had trouble getting them to send transcripts bearing my new name. Therefore I was underemployed for many years because I could not prove that I had a college education. Also I could not attend graduate school, or most any college or university, without my undergraduate transcripts.

I was devastated to think that I might never be able to claim the B.S. degree that I'd worked so hard to earn and was still paying for, by the way. I contacted the Registrar's office numerous times by letter and long distance phone calls trying to get them to acknowledge my name change and have my transcripts forwarded, so that I could claim my undergraduate degree and get on with my life.

It took the utmost in faith and character for me to continue to pay my school loans on a degree that I was not even able to claim I'd earned, and might not ever be able to claim, so far as I knew at the time.

But I did continue to pay on my undergraduate school loans, even during those years when I earned less than $5,000.00 per year. I still have the letter from the Illinois State Scholarship Commission dated February 1989, saying that I had paid my loans in full. It took me fourteen years to pay off my undergraduate school loans but I paid every dime.

I also requested from the alumni office at Roosevelt University, a corrected degree, with my new name on it. I briefly mentioned how difficult it had been for me to earn the degree and so therefore I naturally wanted to proudly display it; and that as a matter of fact, I was still paying for the degree.

I was told that such a corrected degree was "entirely out of the question," because "it is a historical document." I argued that a corrected degree was not going to invalidate the historicity of the original degree; and as a matter of fact, I would hang them side by side if they insisted. But I was flatly refused; and after several similar conversations with the registrar's and the alumni office, I put the issue out of my mind.

Finally the day of dread came when a department head at Central Piedmont Community College came to me and said that they must have my college transcripts before my next quarter-to-quarter contract would be renewed. I again made a call to Roosevelt University's Mr. Registrar himself and beseeched him earnestly to please send a transcript with my correct name on it, so that I wouldn't lose my part-time employment as an adjunct instructor.

***

I had my first surgery, a double 36 C mastectomy, during the Christmas break of my first year at Central Piedmont Community College. I pleaded with the surgeon to do it at the outpatient surgery center, because I was paying for everything myself and I couldn't afford to stay in the hospital. He was reluctant but agreed when I assured him that I would have somebody there to drive me home and look after me for several days.

My girlfriend and I lived in Monroe, a town some forty-five minutes away from Charlotte, NC. I was still driving the black-on-grey 1974 Dodge Charger SE that I'd brought with me from Illinois, to work everyday at CPCC in Charlotte. I'd taken excellent care of it and it ran great, but its V-8 engine required plenty of gasoline. We lived in Monroe to be close to her job.

The surgery went well, but post-operatively, I had

185

trouble with low blood pressure. As a matter of fact, I was delayed in leaving the outpatient surgery center because I couldn't even sit up without passing out. It was no small amount of tissue that was excised that morning, and I was low on my intravascular volume. One of the physicians kept taking my blood pressure, and each time he'd look at me, trying to conceal his alarm and say, "Are you all right?"

Finally after several attempts, they packed me up, pinning my JP (Jackson-Pratt) drains up under my arms, to the surgical dressing that was wrapped around my upper torso. All this was then packed in under my flight jacket, which was zipped up tight. I was then loaded into a wheelchair and dumped outside by myself, as my girlfriend had gone to some distant parking lot to get the car. It was about 4:30 on a Friday afternoon; and I was the last patient out. The staff was anxious to go home.

As we rode down Independence Boulevard in the rush hour traffic, I was so weak and lightheaded that I could hardly sit up, but I was euphoric to have the surgery completed. I recall that my senses were acutely perceptive. The noise of the traffic seemed unbearably loud and more chaotic than usual, and the lights were uncomfortably bright.

Just after we got home, my girlfriend chose that time to inform me that she was leaving me for another lover; and she left immediately. For the next several days, I struggled to take care of myself. Every time I'd stand up, the room would go black in front of me. I was not able to make it into the kitchen at the other end of the house. I knew that I needed to eat or at least drink something.

So I thought to get out of bed and immediately get down onto the floor; then I wormed my way into the kitchen being careful not to put too much stress on the scores of subcutaneous and cutaneous sutures and staples. When I got to the kitchen, I'd get up for a few seconds in order to find something to eat or drink. As soon as I began to feel faint, I'd quickly get back down on the floor again, lie there and wait for the spell to pass. Over the next several days, it usually took several respites down on the floor like that to accomplish this feeding task. In this manner, however, I was able to get enough hydration and some nourishment to the extent that the fainting spells abated and I was well on my way to recovery.

I didn't know anyone in Monroe, since we'd only lived there a couple of months and I worked everyday in the city. I would not have been able to drive myself back to the hospital and I'm certain that I wouldn't have called an ambulance.

I had just a short time to recuperate before I was due back at work after the New Year. I spent that time alone, without hearing from another soul the entire three weeks.

I had a puppy-cat named Felix who I'd brought with me from Illinois. Somebody had dumped him out as a kitten in my driveway and I'd noticed him around the garbage cans. One day when I had opened the garage door, he darted in and so I took him upstairs and fed him. He ate heartily and purred with gratitude, and wanted to stay with me and so he did. He was unusually lovable and not as independent as most cats by nature seem to be.

He seemed more dog than cat: he'd walk on a leash for me and rode in my car with no problems. Wherever I was in the house, he was always on top of me. If I was sitting at the table writing, he'd come and sit on top of my papers as though he liked to make them rattle. He liked for me to talk to him, and in reply, he'd twitch his ears, cock his head and trill contently. He stayed on top of my feet or on my lap during this Christmas time. He seemed to sense that

187

I needed him and he was always nearby. I was grateful for his companionship and I would have been unbearably lonely without him. What a beloved gift from God was my pet Felix. I will never forget him.

During this time, I received a letter from *Science of Mind* magazine notifying me that my article, "How I Quit Smoking," would be published in the January 1984 issue, and it was. This was my first magazine publication, and I recognized that this good news, coming at this particular time, was divine encouragement which in addition to Felix, gave me hope and sustained me through this very lonely valley.

My girlfriend didn't come back, and I immediately realized that I had to move out of the house because I couldn't afford the rent and expenses alone even for one month, and neither could she. Our house was filled with plenty of good furniture, including a piano that I'd bought for myself upon college graduation. The furniture was mine and I'd moved it all in the yellow truck, from my Illinois apartment, where I'd accumulated it over five years at a much higher income. I knew that I could not afford a place large enough to hold all the furniture. I couldn't even afford to move the furniture again.

Soon I realized that I had to be recuperated from my surgery and be moved out of the house by the time I was due back at work just after the New Year. I swung into action.

I called a Unitarian minister acquaintance in Charlotte and asked him if he knew of any elderly parishioner within his congregation who might like a young man to live with him or her.

He said, "I might have an angle on that; let me get back to you."

Lucky for me, he called back soon to tell me of an elderly lady he knew who was interested in meeting me. I drove to her home on Sharon View Road in

Charlotte. She had a lovely home in an excellent location; and getting to work at CPCC would be an easy, straight shot up Providence Road.

Mrs. Hanson was up in her eighties, able to get around fairly well in her house, and was mentally intact. She was obviously of excellent breeding and considering her social skills, she struck me as probably having attended finishing school. She was prim and proper, and a gifted conversationalist. I marveled at how well she and the likes of me seemed to talk effortlessly for easy lengths of time. She loved to have tea and sweets in the evening and she seemed to look forward to our several visits before I moved in. She told me she craved peanut butter and confided that sometimes she ate it right out of the jar.

She invited me to move in and I was delighted. I couldn't have been happier with the arrangement; she had a lovely home in an excellent neighborhood close to my job, and the rent was only $35.00 per week. I was happy to be back in Charlotte, where I would have many more social and career opportunities. There was a running track at the nearby Country Day School where I'd be able to continue my running.

Now I had a place to live; but what to do with all my furniture? I realized that I had to sell it or give it all away; there was no room at Mrs. Hanson's lovely home. I called the owner of the local furniture store; he was interested and came to my house to take a look. He bought everything including the piano. I was sorry to see it all go, especially my piano.

But worst of all, I had to get rid of my cat, Felix. He would not be allowed at Mrs. Hanson's house. I was lucky to find a veterinarian to take Felix, and even though I knew he'd have the best of care, it just about killed me to give him up. Felix had been my best buddy for about ten years.

So, that's what I did over my Christmas vacation of 1983.

***

The living arrangement with Mrs. Hanson was mutually beneficial and satisfying, but unfortunately she died in her sleep several years later. I found her dead in her bed, in the morning as I was leaving for work. I immediately called her family with the sad news. She had been like a grandmother to me; we'd had many pleasant conversations. Quite honestly, she was my closest friend at the time. I was so saddened by the loss of her. I was just not ready for her to die.

Her children were obviously glad that "she was finally gone," and ordered me out of the house immediately, so that they could "quickly get the house sold." Their unlovely attitude towards their mother's death astonished me, and I was appalled at their unkindness to me. I had done many favors to help take care of Mrs. Hanson, who was entirely housebound.

Once again, I was out of a home in the blink of an eye. Mrs. Hanson's folks were adamant that I move out within the week! And so I moved in with an older couple who lived in nearby Matthews, for about a month, until I could get into an apartment back in Charlotte.

17. Quiet Desperation

The mass of men lead lives of quiet desparation.

Thoreau, *Walden,*
Chapter 1-A Economy, 9

In the meantime, I'd found another girlfriend and after dating for a couple of years, we were married in May 1986. We had a lovely church wedding at St. Christopher's, she in a handmade white, lacey gown and veil; and I wore tails. Her four siblings and their families all came from Michigan. I hired a chauffeur driven 1976 Silver Shadow Rolls Royce to drive us to our honeymoon hotel.

I was still instructing at Central Piedmont Community College, and at the same time I had continued to stay close to my faith, indeed church-related activities comprised my entire social life. I volunteered at Mercy Hospital, in the pastoral services department, because I was testing out my discernment for a hospital ministry.

My math instructing experience had brought out my communication abilities and also my gift for empathizing with people, gaining their trust and rapport. This in addition to my devotion to my faith, my lifelong exposure to, study of, and love of Judeo-Christian teachings, and the example of my grandfather, all caused me to consider professional Christian ministry.

An opportunity came for me to attend seminary as a postulant for the priesthood and so I resigned at Central Piedmont Community College, and my wife and I moved to upstate New York.

At the seminary, we postulants lived a "modified

191

rule of life," wearing long black cassocks resembling monks, even when we went into town. We lived together in a monastery setting; the seminary was in an old Tudor-style building, previously a tuberculosis sanitarium. We ate together in a refectory, attended early morning mass, noon prayers, and evening prayers seven days a week.

In addition to our studies, we each had an outside vocation. I had come to seminary with a well-established hospital ministry in Charlotte; and so I worked at the same New York hospital where my wife was employed as an RN, in the pre-op and post-op holding areas. This was to be a ministry to surgical patients with the idea that "God is everywhere with you, even in the operating room."

I really got into the monastery life. I enjoyed the contemplative life, the meditative solitude, the library, and the chapel. As you might suppose, I soaked up my studies and was the top student in my small class. I enjoyed everything, but particularly enjoyed studying the Bible from the literary and historical point of view. Much to my surprise, I also excelled in Greek and we learned to read the New Testament in Greek.

We were trained in the priest-craft, liturgy, homiletics, and hermeneutics of the Anglican Catholic tradition. Using the 1928 Prayer Book and the 1940 Hymn Book, we were trained in the style and manner of priests hundreds of years ago.

In preparation for seminary, I was asked to produce my Certificate of Baptism. I had some recollection of my mother mentioning my baptism in Ohio, just before they moved to Chicago. My father was an ordained Methodist minister with an appointment at a nearby small-town church when I was born, as it says on my original birth certificate. My grandfather was also an ordained Methodist minister and had been all his life.

There is not a more pleasurable duty for a minister to perform than an infant baptism; especially the baptism of his own child or grandchild, and so I had never in my life doubted that I'd been baptized. As a young man, a postulant for the priesthood, with precious few connections to my childhood, I very much wanted my baptismal certificate. So for this reason, at age thirty-five, I attempted to contact my mother. I found her in an institution and wrote her letter after letter, requesting the details of my baptism, but she didn't reply.

Finally I did receive a very short note from her written in a huge scrawl, like a child's handwriting. She said only: "You were never baptized. Your father wanted a boy. Remember?" That was it; I still have the letter.

And yes, I believed her. I never knew my mother to lie; she might do anything she could to avoid telling the truth, but she never lied in all the time I knew her. Besides, I experienced a shock of recognition that what she had said was true.

Did that ever hit me! I'd always thought I'd been baptized. I could not believe that two ordained ministers consciously decided not to baptize their first child and grandchild. What a low blow which at thirty-five years old hurt worse than ever. To think that I could still, after all these years of successfully surviving my parents, suffer from their cruelty. *God! When was I ever going to be free of them?*

But most of all, her words confirmed my deepest intuition over the years: one of the reasons my father despised me was that I had been born a girl. All the rejection and hate I'd felt from him as a child had been real. I had not imagined any of it. This was an excellent, though painful and late, confirmation of my insight into my childhood.

193

Now, I realize that for many people, there is no particular meaning attached to having, or not having their child baptized. If they choose not to baptize their child, it doesn't mean that the parents love their child any less, and it certainly doesn't mean that their child's soul will go to hell. I realize that many think this baptism stuff is all a bunch of hooey.

But for many others however, to decide not baptize your child is nearly a sin or a crime, certainly a terrible rejection of the child and a sign of serious parental neglect. To have a child, yet not think him worthy of the sacrament of baptism, an act of dedicating the child to God and a symbol of the child's entering God's kingdom, when you as a parent believe in such and were yourself baptized, is to me a despicable act of rejection. And in the context of my childhood, not baptizing me was very much a conscious act of rejection.

I immediately went to a priest. Here I was a postulant for the priesthood, confirmed in the church but never baptized. Technically speaking, not being baptized was an absolute disqualification to be a priest. Even Jesus was baptized before he began his ministry. I was miserably ashamed, even though I could reason with myself that I shouldn't be.

I told the priest I'd just found out that I'd never been baptized and mentioned that I'd been abandoned as a kid and grew up, for the most part, in a children's home. I did not tell him the stinging words of my mother.

He said all the right things, comforting me. He said, "God's grace is not limited to the acts of man," and things like that, trying to reassure me. But I was adamant; and so in several weeks, I as a type of infant, was baptized along with three other infants in a beautiful cathedral ceremony. It was a supremely spiritual and meaningful event for me. I am so grateful that God is not limited to the thoughts, acts, and prayers of mankind.

***

In the seminary I learned a lot of things in addition to a particular brand of Christianity, the priest craft, and how to enjoy port wine. The ultimate thing that I learned was that I could be more useful to God in the medical profession with my sleeves rolled up, than in the cloister of the church.

I believe that all priests and ministers should also be "tentmakers." That is a reference to the apostle Paul, and is a way of saying that clergy should have a means of supporting themselves independent of the church. And I certainly wasn't going to be a priest because I "couldn't do anything else," which is how some people regard full-time priests and ministers.

But I didn't act on this immediately; I tested it for at least another year. I got permission from my bishop to leave the seminary, to return home and "read for orders," which meant completing the requirements by independent study. This was my way of leaving the seminary, but not closing every door behind me, although when I left, I had every intention of getting into the medical field.

So I left the seminary after completing half the program and I returned to Asheville, North Carolina because, as it was planned by my bishop, that was the town in which I was to have started a new church after completing seminary. There I served at the altar of St. Mary's Church seven days a week for Evening Prayers and Mass, while working concurrently at Memorial Mission Hospital as a nursing assistant in the neurosurgery ward.

My wife who was an RN, had four physicians, a

195

physician assistant and other medical professionals in her family; and they encouraged me to consider a career as a physician assistant.

During the year before PA school, I continued to work at the local hospital as a nursing assistant and also took chemistry and anatomy courses at AB Technical College.

I started PA training at Wake Forest University School of Medicine the following August, 1989. I commuted there weekly, one hundred and fifty miles, returning home Friday and then driving back to the medical center early Monday morning. I did this so that my wife could keep her nursing job in Asheville, as she wished. Also, we had planned to settle in that lovely, western North Carolina town after I finished PA school.

Once again, I contacted an area minister in Winston-Salem, asking if he knew of an elderly parishioner near the medical center who might rent a room to me during the week. Such an elderly lady was easy to find in his parish. I as a thirty-seven-year old married man and medical student had no problem in finding another arrangement such as I had had with Mrs. Hanson years earlier.

I had borrowed more than $30,000 for my PA medical training. I was utterly fatigued from trying to get my life and my career established and I wanted to get a job, settle down, and finally be able to buy my own home.

I was convinced that I, at least as much as any other person I knew, was truly "called" to the medical profession. Every experience in my life so far had brought me to this point and would contribute, I thought, to my ability to be (my definition of) a good healthcare provider. Of that I was utterly convinced.

I had finally paid off my undergraduate school loans as late as February 1989. Before that, I was not able to borrow money to attend graduate school. I had also finally been successful in getting my university transcripts sent from Roosevelt University with my correct name on them. So in 1989, at age thirty-seven, and after much wasted time, I was finally able to move forward with graduate school education and my life.

My wife was not doing well, and I became increasingly worried about her while I was away during the week at school. She seemed to have sunk into a deep depression. She'd go for a week without taking a shower and would have gone longer if I hadn't begged her to take a shower. She became withdrawn and gained a lot of weight.

At the same time, I was utterly buried in schoolwork. I was so worried about her during the week that I could hardly concentrate on my studies; the tension escalated intensely. I felt she was slipping right before my eyes, but I absolutely had to finish school; and the pressure on me became acute.

When I finally graduated from PA school in August 1991, it was the crowning achievement of my life, the biggest relief and my happiest day by far. My brother and sister were there, along with my wife's family. They had all traveled long distances to attend my graduation. The pictures taken, which I still have, show me a euphorically happy and healthy young man with my wife, brother, sister and wife's family. I have a photograph of me with my niece, Megan, than nine months old, and my wife's nephew of about the same age. I have photographs of myself with classmates, instructors, and the director of the program, and even a patient of mine who drove from Knoxville, because she "just wanted to come to my graduation and bring me a gift."

Just a couple of days after my PA graduation ceremony, the first graduation ceremony of mine I'd ever attended, I got a package in the mail from Roosevelt University. It was my Bachelor of Science degree bearing the original date of my graduation, and best of all it had my new name on it! I had long since given up on getting them to reissue me a new degree with my corrected name on it. But eight years later it serendipitously came to me in the mail. At the age of thirty-nine, in less than one week, I had received two different degrees. Finally I was employable and I dared to dream of soon being able to finally buy my own home. All I needed was to pass my certifying exam, but it would be possible for me to start a job while I was waiting to sit for the exam. Finally, I was on my way to getting a job and getting my own home.

***

Even so, my wife was still depressed and didn't share in my joy. At the time, I didn't understand why she wasn't happy, as I had finally finished school and would be getting a job soon. As a matter of fact, she became increasingly depressed, more slovenly in her hygiene, doing and saying things which were inappropriate and out of character.

She'd suddenly run out the door, leaving the stove on. She'd lash out at me, accusing me of having affairs with other women. She increasingly blew up at me, stormed out of the apartment and would be gone for days. I'd never hear from her during those absences and when she came back, she'd rage at me when I'd ask her where she'd been. As I'd spent the last couple of years mostly gone from home, I had no idea who her friends were and where she might go.

I became greatly concerned as to how she was able to hold down her nursing job. She was acting so crazy that I became urgent to find a job, in accordance with my survivor instincts. I was reeling with trying to figure out what was wrong with her, but as I'd done so many times in my life before, I focused my efforts on what I urgently needed to do, which was to get a job as soon as I could. I began job hunting with feverish intensity. And after I found a job, I'd planned to cram for the certifying exam, which I'd already registered and paid for.

One day, I found several pills in her pocket. They were not in a typically labeled pharmacy container, but were just loose in her pocket. I asked her where she got the pills and what she was taking them for. I confronted her with my suspicion that she was using illicit drugs, maybe even stealing them from the drug cart at the hospital, especially in light of her increasingly unusual and volatile behavior. She went berserk and again went raging out of the apartment yelling and cursing. This was most uncharacteristic; I'd never before heard her curse or use vulgar words. My wife had always been a very religious and overly pious person. Again she was gone for days; I tried not to worry and continued with my job hunting.

I felt my scalp crawl as I remembered how shocked I was also at my mother's unpredictable, violent and volatile behavior, her uncharacteristic cursing and swearing, as she also deteriorated before my eyes, just before we were sent to the Children's Home.

***

On the Labor Day weekend of 1991, I had been sitting at the kitchen table typing résumé's all day; it had been just two weeks since I'd graduated from PA school. This was the fifth day that my wife had been gone. There was a knock on the door.

I opened the door to a couple of police officers. My

heart fell; something must have happened to my wife. They handed me a very legal-looking paper and said, "I'm sorry, sir, but we are here to carry out this Judge's order to evict you from your home."

I was stunned; I couldn't comprehend what in the world they were talking about. I stuttered and stammered, "What do you mean? What is this all about?" I was typically polite and offered no resistance; I invited the officers into the apartment.

They explained that they had an *Ex Parte* eviction order from a Judge to put me out of the apartment instantly. I stood dumbfounded; they handed me the paper. They explained that it had been initiated by my wife. I asked them, "Why?" They explained that there didn't have to be any reason—that she could simply go to a judge and obtain this *Ex Parte* eviction at any time, with absolutely no evidence, and no witness. She needn't say anything other than that she "feared for her safety."

I looked at the paper; sure enough it was signed by a judge whose name I recognized. It was a one-page, brief and simple form. My wife had filled out her name and our address on the top. There was one sentence which asked: "Why are you seeking this?" There was only one tiny space in which she, the plaintiff, was to fill in the blank. There was my wife's handwriting scrawled all over the paper and in the margins; it was mostly illegible. There were numerous incomplete sentences, misspelled words, crossed-out words and phrases. Her handwriting looked like that of a child's, a person on drugs, or a mentally ill person. What she had written made no sense at all.

I felt my skin crawl. Her insane, unsubstantiated, uncorroborated blathering was all it took to ruin my life? I couldn't believe it. She indicated on the form that she was afraid for her safety; though she offered no evidence of violence. She offered no rational reason for her plea, just as the officer had earlier said, no reason was required.

One thing she wrote I will never forget. She gave as the reason she feared for her safety, was because I had been beaten and abused as a child by my father, "his father tried to kill him" she wrote; and that I was abandoned as a child and had grown up in a children's home.

It was obvious to me that she'd been coached by someone to do this. She'd never have known how to go before a Magistrate to obtain an *Ex Parte* eviction order. She clearly had someone to coach her on what psychological buzzwords to say as well, such as that since I had been abused as a child, I would therefore abuse her. This was the reason why I should be evicted from my home in a moment's time, with absolutely no evidence. I was speechless.

The officer's were unusually polite, but they said I had to leave immediately, that I could grab just a few personal items in about five minutes time, but that I had to leave with them now and if I ever returned I'd be arrested and thrown in jail.

I said, "Where will I go?"

One of the officers said, "Don't you have any family you can go to?"

"No, I don't."

"Well, maybe you can find a men's homeless shelter to stay at."

They ushered me out of the door and onto the street within few minutes time, just as they'd promised. I just stood and stared for a few seconds. I was absolutely homeless and I had no job. I had no family and no friends in the area. I hadn't spent enough time in the area to develop a network, a circle of friends, since I stayed in Winston-Salem five days a week while attending PA school.

It was about 4:15 p.m. on a Friday afternoon. I got into my Ford Festiva and in a numbing state of shock, I backed it out. I had no idea where I was going. I drove out onto the highway and headed north into town. Something told me to stop at the bank. Sure enough, she'd emptied and closed all our accounts, including a separate account containing thousands of dollars of my school loan money. She'd also emptied out our lockbox. Now, I had no home, no job, and no money.

I got back into my car and drove to the church. This was the cathedral I'd been baptized in a few years earlier, and it was my only connection in town. Lucky for me, the clergy were still there. I told them what had happened. By outward appearances I calm, but I was numb with shock.

As so many times earlier in my life, I knew I had to disassociate myself from the craziness that I'd been subjected to, and focus on dealing with my immediate need which was to find a safe place to stay. I knew I couldn't bear to stay in a homeless shelter; that would have been the end of the line for me.

The deacon was there with her husband. They said, "Well, you will just come home with us." I was so grateful I didn't know how to reply.

The eviction notice also ordered that I was to appear in court in a week to defend myself. Now how is a man supposed to line up a lawyer and a decent suit of clothes to wear to court under such circumstances? The deacon, through other church folk, got me connected to an attorney in town. By the way, I paid all my attorney's fees, not the church.

The attorney said I needed to get several persons to write letters vouching for my good character; and I needed to come up with these letters by the court date. I got two of those letters from the rector of the cathedral and the director of my medical school PA program.

The attorney treated me most disrespectfully, like a common criminal, like the lowest-class piece of white trash on the street. However, he didn't seem to doubt my innocence and knew exactly what had happened. When I asked him how it could possibly be, that I could be thrown out of my own house, with no evidence whatsoever, he mocked me scornfully,

"Of course, you can. Don't you know? That's the oldest trick in the book, and you mean you're so dumb that you don't know about it? What kind of an idiot are you anyway that you should let this kind of thing happen to you?"

Well, that was something I was definitely going to find out, if I ever got myself out of this mess. *Welcome to the world of men,* I thought.

On the appointed day, I showed up at the courthouse with everything in order; the court I was assigned to was packed with people. We waited for four hours, and mine was the last case to be called. After all that waiting, I didn't even appear before the judge, even though I wanted to. My attorney handled everything while I waited alone in another room.

The *Ex Parte* eviction was completely thrown out. There were absolutely no charges or complaints brought against me, and I had never been arrested. My wife was ordered to pay back the school loan money she'd stolen from me. And as far as the court was concerned, that was the end of the issue. Through our attorneys, my wife made overtures suggesting her desire to drop the whole thing and reconcile.

Then my attorney came back to me, in a room where I anxiously awaited alone, and with irritation said, "Now what do you want to do?" He made no effort to hide the fact that he was bored with the whole thing, anxious to be done with the whole mess and eager to get the hell out of there.

I thought, *Geez, bud, this is my life that you don't give a damn about being ruined.*

I was livid. I thought, *Thank-you very much society, for once again nearly ruining my entire life. Now the fun and games are over, and I'm just supposed to forget it all?*

I said, "Are you kidding? I don't play these kinds of games. The marriage is over; I will never have anything to do with her again."

So then he suggested that we immediately proceed with a legal separation, to which I readily agreed. And so, in less than an hour, our six-year-old marriage was entirely ripped apart by the aggravated lawyer who was anxious to get the hell out of there. The equal distribution part was easy because I said I wanted only my personal things and nothing else. So once again, I gave up all my furniture, including yet another piano. Later, after the mandatory law of one year continuous separation had elapsed, our divorce was final.

***

In the meantime, the date to sit for my certification exam came while I was still living at the clergy's home and before I could get moved out. Therefore I didn't have any of my school books or papers and so I couldn't study, and wouldn't have been able to concentrate anyway.

I requested to cancel my registration and reschedule for a later time when I was emotionally and mentally prepared. I was told I could do that, but the $500.00 registration fee would not be refunded. So I sat for the exam. I just barely flunked it, and so I had to retake it—and repay for it again.

Even with all that, I was able to find a job in just a couple of weeks. I grabbed the first job I could find. I didn't want to take advantage of my clergy hosts; so I wanted to get out of their home as soon as possible. I took my first job as a PA in October 1991, at the local health department. My salary was $28,000 per year. When I started my job, I knew that I was more vulnerable than I'd ever been in my life; and as usual, I had no support and no safety net. It was all I could do to focus on one day at a time and not be disabled with anger and depression.

Then I found an apartment within walking distance of my job. When I moved my personal things out of what had been our apartment, I insisted for my own protection that a police officer and several others accompany me. I wouldn't consider being alone with her ever again, and this time I was going to make the law work on my behalf. I rented a small do-it-yourself moving truck; and the deacon, her daughter, son, and I moved my things out.

Again, she made a few feeble overtures indicating her interest in reconciliation (or something). This was communicated to me in ways that none of the other people there could have understood, except her and me. But I moved my books, clothing, and personal things out as quickly as I could. I know of many things that I left behind. I got out of there and out of her life as fast as I possibly could, and I have never looked back. Never.

***

Now, I will tell you, from the vantage point of twelve years after this happened, that there was never a time in my life when I was closer to losing it. I was outraged at a society that had a provision for such a thing to happen to me. After staying out of trouble and working my ass off for thirty-nine years, so that I wouldn't be "a burden on society," I then experienced the possibility of having all my life's efforts completely destroyed by the flimsiest whim of a crazy woman. That was more than I could accept.

And I didn't give a damn that "for some, this law is very much needed." I had absolutely had it! I wanted to say, "Fuck you society! Fuck you, fuck you, and fuck everyone." I wanted to find that judge and tear him apart. I would have loved to find a way to get his irresponsible, fucking fat ass thrown out of his home and into the street, and see how he liked to have his life ruined.

Why should I bust my ass trying to be a solid citizen? Why should I bust my ass trying to get my life straightened out? At thirty-nine years old, my life had been nothing but a struggle and I was sick, sick, and sick of it!

I wanted to say, "You fucking assholes have picked the wrong damn person to throw out on the street. I have been thrown out just once too damn many times." Years and years of abuse were roaring in my ears and I felt the top of my head would explode. I was incensed; but as in all my prior life, I kept my feelings to myself and I didn't say a word.

To know that my wife could go to a judge and get me literally thrown out of my house into the street, using the reason that I had been abandoned, abused, and beaten as a child, is an absolute outrage! It's not enough that I had to endure this horror as a child, but at thirty-nine years old, I had to have it shoved into my face as the *reason* why I should *again* be abused!

Sorry, folks, but that's just not any society that I wanted to have anything to do with. That's just too much for me to take. Call it cowardice; call it whatever you want. I knew that I was not a coward; I'd had too many opportunities in life to prove to myself that I had any necessary courage. But I just could not accept living in such a shit-hole society.

I absolutely understand why some people choose to drop out of society. Everyone has their limit. You don't think you do? I assure you, I can find ways to put you at your limit, and push you over the edge.

I know that life's shit can push a person over the edge and make him turn off, drop out, go crazy, or go ballistic. If you see someone beaten down by life's circumstances and you are tempted to think, *why doesn't he just get it together and deal with it?* Don't, because I assure you that you could easily be such a person. There's very little difference between you or me, and such a down-and-out person.

The main difference is that most have enough wealth, connections or family members to hold them up, to carry them along or to even cover for them. But others have no wealth, no connections, no family, no safety net and no hope. And only heaven can help such people who also have poor health and/or intellectual limitations.

Obviously I picked myself up, and continued to move myself along; but I can't tell you how or more importantly why. Maybe so I'd be sure to pay my fucking school bills; heaven forbid that I should ever owe anyone.

I continued to go through the motions of practicing my faith, even though I didn't believe in anything. I finally got to the point where I just said to God, *Okay, about all I can say is that I'm here. You can help me in my unbelief if you'd like, but it won't make much difference to me if you do or you don't.*

After the divorce, I went to my priest, who represented me to the Bishop. As regards my previous marriage, I received a canonical Judgment, the first such in my diocese, according to my priest. This is vaguely similar to an annulment in the Roman Catholic Church, especially in that it would allow me to remarry in the Church at some future time, if I desired.

Even though I wasn't dating anyone and had no plans to remarry, I requested this Judgment because it is my nature to directly confront and deal with all my business, and to leave no loose ends untied.

I also wanted to make a point to the Church that there are in fact some people, even men, who are victims of divorce or victims of marriage; and furthermore it is unfair to disallow such victims the sacrament of a future marriage.

The Church still has a lot of progress to make in becoming less concerned with legalism and more concerned with pastoral care. It took me two years to get this Judgment.

As more years passed by, I came to regard people, marriage, and all of society's institutions with a healthy cynicism. And I hated to admit that I was still vulnerable to getting into a marriage too hastily or staying in a bad one, because of my lifelong existential loneliness, my desire to connect and my wish to make a family for myself, even though I've never had the privilege of producing children.

Even without such vulnerabilities, I knew that most people get married for all the wrong reasons. And frequently they stay in bad marriages not because they "work very hard every day at the marriage," (that's crap) but because they are just too stubborn to throw in their cards, because of financial security within the marriage, or because they are just too damn lazy to make a move.

***

I tried not to become misanthropic, but even in my career life, I began to understand those who've said that the esteem of the medical profession has been debased, from both inside and outside influences, and we let it happen. And come to think of it, many professions are corrupt; that's because many people are. Some people go into the medical profession, the clergy, or other professions, for the perceived prestige or the money, with no other sense of calling.

It was difficult for me to admit that I would not have gotten a job, or even been accepted into medical school if my gender reassignment had been known. It has been difficult for me to soldier on, as if everything is just fine, with this kind of insight. But I have faith that it won't be so difficult for future generations. In the meantime, I have come to regard my transsexualism as a gift, and to hell with what others may think about me.

Even though I felt this ambivalence toward my profession, I knew that I discerned a sense of calling to be in the medical profession. *But on the other hand,* I argued with myself, *who gives a damn about that? That kind of pious thinking will get you nowhere.*

And for the first time, I came to wonder if some who go into the ministry or priesthood, do so because they are spineless cowards, using their collar to protect themselves, or because they couldn't make it in the real world, or because they couldn't do anything else. The church can be a refuge for dysfunctional people, both clergy and laity alike.

Unfortunately my experience has been that most everyone is only out for him or herself, although that is not all bad. When the chips are really down, a truly altruistic person is rare, and some would argue does not exist: "No one is really altruistic; one always has an ulterior motive to altruism, even Mother Theresa."

Within the Church, some people are often more willing to help those who are seem far removed from them—in another church, another neighborhood, or another country. It's too messy to help someone right where you're at, in your own neighborhood, in your own church or, or even at your job. For example, why didn't you Habitat for Humanity folks ever help me get (not give me) a home? I've been right here in the church all my life, and I certainly did ask for help.

Some people will help only those persons to whom they feel superior. I have noticed on a few occasions in my life that people who had "helped me," they later, when they perceived me to have transcended whatever it was that made me seem inferior to them, withdrew their support and even shunned me. They were afraid that I might surpass them somehow. Or their "help" came with the tacit expectation that I toe their party line, and I didn't. It's been difficult to maintain a noble spirit and my faith in people in spite of these my experiences, but I am able to, in part, because of the example of my grandfather's life.

On that day in September 1991 when I was thrown out of my apartment into the street by the police, I was a type of an innocent man. I had been trying all my life to do everything right. I had been trying to prove that I was not a piece-of-shit kid that had been tossed out by his parents—who were aided by society to so easily do. I had worked my ass off to get an education so that I wouldn't be a "burden on society." I had squelched my emotions, trying to prove that my anxieties and my transsexualism were just simple things, so easy to deal with, and certainly nothing with which I'd trouble anyone else, or society at large.

I had never allowed myself the proper time to grieve the loss of my childhood, or any of my losses. I had been trying to prove that all those childhood

210

abuses wouldn't stop me from being a solid, upright, productive citizen. And I did successfully prove that.

I was always trying not to offend anyone's sensibilities, trying not to make waves. But why shouldn't I? I didn't give a damn about proving anything to anybody anymore, nor did I give damn about "what others might think" about me.

I began to detest that past tendency in me to be too concerned about "what others might think." But I also realized that it had been an aspect of my past survival behavior. I realized that an innocent man in this society is pathetic and disgusting. An innocent man is never really respected by men or women, no matter what they say. I would make sure that I was no longer an innocent man. No more Mr. Nice Guy. "Nice guys finish last," as Leo Durocher had said.

I started noticing men who were considered by their peers to be assholes and a pain in the neck; and it occurred to me that I could learn some valuable lessons from these types of guys. Interestingly, they always got what they wanted and they didn't give a damn what anyone thought about them. What a tremendous freedom. Life was just a damn sport; so why not have some fun?

I watched them and started to take some serious lessons. I looked for every opportunity to stand up for myself, to demand my due, to express my unpopular opinion, to firmly persist, persist, persist, no matter how exasperated anyone became. To be assertive or aggressive if need be, to risk being perceived as an asshole. I didn't care what anyone thought of me and the truth is: when you have that attitude, people respect you more, not less. It was an unusual exhilaration and wonderful fun.

For example, I went on a couple of job interviews that I knew I had absolutely no interest in. I practiced a very "Fuck you, I'm totally self-confident" attitude.

What great sport; I loved it. As you might imagine, most of these interviews went well and I got offers. What fun it was to reject someone, anyone, after I'd been rejected bazillions of times before in my life.

I don't have children or anyone dependent on me. Why should I care, for what reason, for what purpose? Why did I carry on, instead of dropping out of society? Maybe I can't give you any good reason; and I won't offer any pious bullshit explanation, other than to say that I was curious to see what would happen next. Maybe I kept on so that I could one day tell you this story, as I am doing now.

After I settled into my Asheville job and apartment, I wrote a detailed, four page letter to my state representative about my experience with, and opinion of the so-called *Ex Parte* eviction law. I received no reply.

***

The following poem was influenced by my experience of Winslow Homer's famous painting "The Fox Hunt", and also by William Stafford's poem, "Traveling through the Dark." It expresses the idea that many people, like animals, can readily smell another person's vulnerability. And like a shark is attracted to blood in the water, some will prey on your vulnerability if they can find a way to.

212

Eye of the Shaman

The air was hot and still
and I came upon a clearing
naked of trees.
In the parched grass
a doe was standing motionless, alone.
She turned and focused huge heavy eyes on me.
She knows something, what does she know?
She knows everything she needs to know.
Tell me doe, what do you know?
Squinting, I saw the sky moving up high.
She started to move forward, hesitating.
Why doesn't she run from me, what's the matter?
She faltered and tumbled forward onto her knees.
Ah, she's in trouble—
I noticed her heaving flanks,
the sky swirling flapping black.
She couldn't get up, she couldn't go on
and tumbled onto her side.
Her baby was coming—
Instantly she was covered with
chortling black flapping wings
ripping red divots of flesh
from her swollen belly
and the baby still trying to come.
She never struggled against them
but weakly lifted her head to watch,
then lowered it again in resignation.
I raised the gleaming, sweet-smelling barrel
to my shoulder and took aim.
Once again she raised her restless head.
It was then I squeezed the trigger—
then the black flapping screeching chaos
The smack back of the stock against my cheek
The smell of sulfur
The ringing in my ears.

213

Part Seven

Return to Time Travel in the New Millennium (2000)

18. Ringing the Last Bell of Recollection

And so it's taken me all these pages to give you some sense of how I felt driving back to Woodstock in my Mercedes thirty years after my high school graduation there, while listening to the transcendent music of Kitaro's *Silk Road*. I couldn't have been more exhilarated if I'd have come in on *Air Force One*.

All these memories and many more were popping off like firecrackers in my mind as I approached Woodstock's city limits from the south, traveling north on Route 47.

Those old roadside welcome signs I described in Chapter One, "Welcome to Woodstock. No radar. No timers. We don't rely on gadgets. We count on you. Please drive carefully," were gone.

McHenry County used to be Illinois' biggest dairy producing county when I lived there, but no longer is. A herd of black and white Holsteins, or a herd of brown and white Guernsey cows grazing in a green field, is still the most soothing sight I can imagine.

I recalled where the old A & W Root Beer stand used to be, on the west side along Route 47; and I recalled The Timbers restaurant, which used to be on the northwest corner of Routes 47 and Bypass 14.

Traveling on into town, I saw that the Coach Light Inn Pizza place was no longer on the right, on Lake Street, and that McDonald's had come at last to Woodstock. When I lived in Woodstock, we had to drive to Crystal Lake to the nearest McDonald's and we frequently did.

I drove to the square, the tires of my new Mercedes rumbling over the brick street just as the tires on my 1965 drop-top Volkswagen did thirty-five years ago. I parked the car, got out and walked around. Of the stores on the square that I remembered, Frame's Men's Store and Knuth's Sporting Goods Store were still there. And the Elks Club was still across Cass Street from the Jailhouse.

The Home State Bank, where I'd gotten the loan to buy my Volkswagen in 1968, was still on the square but no longer on Benton Street. This bank is now at a different location, in the old Post Office building, and the words "United States Post Office" are still inscribed in the stonework across the top of this faithful, red-brick building.

Across the street is a similar red-brick building; the cornerstone reads 1906. The sign in front says "City Hall." The building appears to be housing the Woodstock Police Department, as I saw officers going in and out, and squad cars parked along the side.

The Opera House is still at the same place on the square but now has a more modern facade. The post office and the "cop shop," as we used to call it, are no longer located on the square. The courthouse and jail and other government facilities have moved to new buildings north of town on Route 47. But all the old buildings on, and in the vicinity of the historic square, still remain.

The Roman Catholic, First Methodist, Free Methodist, Unitarian, Christian Scientist, and St. Ann's Episcopal Churches are all still in the same locations.

Montgomery Ward's, which used to be adjacent to the post office building and where I'd bought my first record player, was gone. The old movie theatre on Main Street was still there, but Stompanato's Barber Shop, which used to be across the street from it, was gone. The train station remains, but it is no longer the Chicago and North Western. Now it's part of the Metra system.

Wayne's Lanes, the bowling alley in the movie

Groundhog Day, is still at the same location on Church Street, just east of the train station. Wayne's Lanes was on my walk to and from school, and it was nice to see it still there.

Going out of town from the west side of the square, up the hill on South Street, I drove to Woodstock Community High School and found it looking exactly the same; however there was a construction site on the front corner of the property. I drove into the broad circle driveway in front of the school, parked my Mercedes right in front, and walked in through the front door. I think the "Welcome to Woodstock High School, Home of the Woodstock Blue Streaks" painted overhead on the archway just inside the door must be the same as when I attended in the late sixties.

Heading out of town on the same road, I drove to the City Park, now called Emricson Park. In the front of the park was where the annual July 4th fireworks display was held. Just inside the front entrance was the Municipal Pool and it looked exactly the same as I'd remembered. The sign which admonished that "your tag has to be sewn to your swim suit, and not pinned on," was still there. I smiled, remembering that sign and how eager I was to go swimming. I recalled obediently but clumsily sewing the tag onto the lower right edge of my swim suit, as I very much wanted to do everything right so that I could go swimming. And at the back of the park was still the trap shooting range.

Driving back into town towards the old Woodstock Children's Home campus on the opposite end of town, I drove through the familiar five-way intersection, and headed north on Seminary Avenue towards the Home. The route seemed so familiar; and I recalled that I'd walked and then later driven through that intersection in my 1965 Volkswagen

218

countless times.

The main building of the Home had been torn down in 1983 and a new building, Hearthstone Village is in its place. The merry-go-round, the softball field and the swings I rode on with Carol were all gone.

We used to play "kick the can" outside behind the old laundry house near the vegetable garden. The old laundry house, where Bud lost his arm, is gone.

The old kitchen, like a heavy-duty camp kitchen with its huge walk-in pantry, walk in freezer, huge stoves, enormous pots and pans, long aluminum-covered table, no-nonsense kitchen utensils such as ladling spoons and tongs—all are gone.

***

As I stood looking at the buildings, I recalled the Home's cook; her name was Dorothy and she was not your stereotypical cook. She and her sister Mildred, who also worked at the Home in the office, were both called "old maids." Miss Dorothy was skinny and sort of a serious, nervous type; she darted around in the kitchen like a hummingbird. She seemed shy around us, but she was a pleasant person and occasionally a smile would break across her uneasy face.

While we were helping her in the kitchen, she tolerated our omnipresent rock and roll music which emanated from our ubiquitous transistor radios. Once after the song "Yesterday" played, she said, "Well, I must admit, that's a very pretty song."

We exclaimed, "That's Paul McCartney of the Beatles! See, our music isn't all bad."

We could tell she was surprised to know that, as she must have thought that all Beatles music was noisy rock and roll junk, without meaningful lyrics. I appreciated this adult who would be honest in her appraisal of our music, and compliment a Beatles song, even if unwittingly.

In the summer, large fans were placed on chairs or on the counters in the kitchen at strategic places, and the exhaust fan in the wall near the ceiling roared with great authority. It amazes me to think how Miss Dorothy lifted all those big cooking pots and pans; however, she did so with the never-ending help of a team of several boys and girls. We all had to help, according to our age, with the food preparation, serving, cleaning up, dishwashing, floor sweeping and mopping. She had a big job to plan and cook two or three meals a day for all those kids and adults. And she had all the cooking timed to come out just right, all at the same time. What an enormous logistical undertaking! But this bird-like woman steered the whole thing.

I recalled the dinner bell; it hung just outside the kitchen window and was attached to a rope which came inside through a knothole. We all wanted a turn to ring that bell, and at precisely fifteen minutes before breakfast, lunch or dinner, she'd give the signal to one of us to ring the bell. We'd get a hold of the rope and snatch it down with a big display of heave-ho. This would tip the cup-shaped bell onto its side, causing the clapper to strike the inside of the large, stone-heavy bell. Then most of the rope's length slithered back outside through the hole, but was caught by the large knot at its end. Then we'd heave it down again for another gong; and so forth many times. Frequently, Miss Dorothy would yell out, trying to constrain her mild exasperation, "Okay, okay, that's enough."

We rang the bell again like that at five minutes before the meal was to begin. By this time, all kids were supposed to be lined up, standing quietly on the other side of our respective closed doors—the boys behind the door on east side of the dining room, and the girls behind the door of the west side of the dining room—both which lead from our dorms into the large noisy dining room. Five minutes later, the last bell was rung and we filed into the dining room.

We were supposed to stand reverently behind our chairs while the house parent said a prayer. At his intonation of "amen," a great clamor of crashing chairs and general chaos broke out as everyone sat down to eat. The exception to this was after we sat down for breakfast. Then we sat dutifully with our hands folded in our laps, listening idly to the house parent read a short morning devotion to us, while watching the steam rise from the large serving bowl of oatmeal.

We rang this bell faithfully seven days a week, three times preceding each meal. You could set your clock by it. I wondered what they ever did with that big bell when the old children's home building was razed.

***

Then I went to the Harrison House building, just below the main building property, where the teenagers had been housed. The exterior building is the same but has been remodeled inside to accommodate the offices of the Christian Life Children's Day Care Center.

The present Day Care Center building is on the field behind the Harrison House where Mr. Beatty used to pull us around in the snow, our sleds attached to either side of the back of his old red Ford pick-up truck. As I stood staring at the new building

221

recalling the snow-laden fields of my childhood, I heard the sounds of the present day kiddies playing outside, as we did years ago on snow sleds or at softball in the summer.

The upstairs back of the Harrison House, the northeast side of the building, used to be the girls dorm. There was the window which opened onto the roof of the brick carport. That window is at the end of the hallway of what used to be the girl's dorm. The metal gate covering that window is still there; it was put over the window in the sixties, to prevent the girls from sneaking out in the middle of the night.

I walked around to the south end of the building and saw the porch swing, still there on the brick and concrete veranda. I walked up the steps and sat on the swing, recalling how we'd spent many summer evenings here whiling away the time and trying to feel a breeze. Now, I was most gratified to find the old Children's Home property in excellent condition, and very well kept up.

I walked around to the front door, finding a sign that reads "Woodstock Christian Life Services." I opened the door, recalling its signature slamming sound of old. Just inside, the entry way had been remodeled to open it up more. When I lived there, several squeaking steps brought you up to a landing. To the left were stairs which led up to the boys' dorm. On the right used to be a small room used as a Chapel; it is now an office.

Straight ahead, there used to be a small hallway, still with creaking floors, and on the right, a pay phone with an inset bench, which we had to use to make personal phone calls.

When I lived there, every board of the dark wooden flooring creaked, now the whole place is carpeted.

On the left of this hallway, at the front left corner of the building, was a sitting room, and then beyond

222

that, extending all along the north side of the building facing the parking lot, were Mr. and Mrs. Beatty's staff quarters.

At the end of this short, dark hallway there used to be the main living room. On your left are stairs which lead upstairs to what used to be the girls' dorm; now the upstairs rooms are used as offices. The steps continue downstairs to where our eating area in the basement used to be. This room was dominated by a large, round, wooden table and the room doubled as our study hall. A large tile-floored rumpus room, which used to have an old bowling machine in it, and our laundry room were also in the basement. However, I did not go downstairs during my visit.

The main living room is still a lovely room. It seemed smaller than I'd remembered it. Its white stucco walls and wood trim have been carefully preserved. The room is trimmed with dark wood wainscoting, baseboards, crown molding and ceiling beams.

The living room still has the three sets of double doors: one leads out onto the south veranda, where the porch swing is; and another leads into what used to be the house parent's living room. The brick fireplace on the east wall of the old house parent's living room has been replaced with a more modern one. The third set of double doors leads into a room which was the house parent's office, and today is also used as an office.

In this office, there is a foot-square cut-out in the wall, located near the south end of the wall, about four foot up from the floor. It is wood-framed and obviously planned for some purpose. This wall cut-out has been there for as long as I can remember. On the other side of the wall of this office, in the right corner of the building, had been the Chapel.

***

By this time, my presence was noted by several of the administrative staff. A woman of mature age approached me. She was impeccably and conservatively groomed, polite and cordial, but with just an edge of reserve; she was so utterly typical of the Free Methodist Church women I recalled.

I introduced myself and told her that I had lived in the Home in the sixties. As I'm accustomed to doing, I immediately intuited that she doubted I looked old enough to have lived anywhere in the sixties. I made it a point to state various facts and other things which would tend to persuade her that I'd really lived there, and that I wasn't an imposter.

It seemed as though I was successful because she became more animated, asking me questions which then made me feel somewhat uneasy, such as: when did I live in the Home, did I know such and such person—all she named I of course did. But if I'd have said so, that would have led to more questioning such as: in what connection did I know such and such person, and what now was my profession and employment, and so forth. I knew that as soon as she knew my name and year of high school graduation, there would be any number of persons she could ask about my identity. And I knew that any person she might ask, including classmates or fellow Home kids would rightly deny ever having heard of me.

I wanted to walk through every room and just stand and stare, allowing any and all memories to flash through my mind without distraction. It was most difficult to stand, maintain appropriate eye contact and chat superficially with her while so many memories of years long past were lit by every sight, sound and smell, like a wrought-iron rack of votive candles in my mind. I wanted to be alone and stay mesmerized by these flickering memories for just awhile, instead of having to move along.

She toured me around through the main level and upstairs; I tried to concentrate on all my eyes could take in, while at the same time engaging in polite conversation; this was a most intense experience. How strange it seemed to be toured through my old Home by a skeptical stranger. She seemed delighted in my telling her any historical detail about the building and she seemed not to know such detail as where the boys' dorm, the girls' dorm, and the staff quarters had been.

When we came back to the main living room, there was a young male administrator who joined us. Finding out the nature of my visit, he said, pointing to the square cut-out in his office, "We've always wondered what this was for. Do you know?"

"Oh yes," she chimed in, "we've all wondered. Whatever is that for?"

I was ashamed to tell them that I didn't know. Even though I'd remembered it being there when I'd lived in the Home, I didn't know its purpose or why it was there. Then I worried they might again revisit the notion that I was an imposter. Funny, when I lived there, I never gave it much thought. Now I was racking my brain, but I couldn't remember ever knowing.

I wondered briefly if it could have been the way sacraments were conveyed back and forth from a sacristy into the Chapel. This, however, would have been a purpose before my time of living in the Home. But no, that didn't seem right; it was a far too liturgical explanation for a Free Methodist or even a Presbyterian chapel.

The building was called Grace Hall when owned

by the (Presbyterian) Todd Seminary for Boys, before it was bought by the Woodstock Children's Home. The purpose of the square cut-out in the wall certainly was known by those boys who lived there before the Seminary closed in 1954.

Maybe someone reading this will know the purpose of that strange, square, framed cut-out hole in the wall.

***

Just south of the Harrison House, and across the lawn is the only other extant building of the Todd School campus. When I lived in the Home, the building was known as the Masonic Temple, and it seemed to be vacant all of the time. One Christmas, the Home had a big dinner in this building for us kids, the staff and their families, and many guests from the nearby Free Methodist Church, which we were required to attend services three times a week.

I guess I looked fairly conspicuous driving up in a new Mercedes, walking around the building, and taking pictures. A man in the front on a riding lawn mower, probably overcome with curiosity, drove over to me, cut the noisy thing off and introduced himself.

What luck; he was the owner of the building. I told him who I was and why I was there, the same way I'd told the woman at the old Harrison House building earlier. As I expected, he also seemed skeptical, thinking I looked too young to have lived in a teenagers' building in the sixties.

I walked to the front door of the building and pointed out the Masonic Temple emblem and masonry just to the lower right of the front door. I then pointed out the cornerstone dated 1910 at the lower left corner of the building. I described to him how the inside of the building looked when I was there. Instead of being two stories, the great hall had been a cavernous room with a soaring ceiling. The large arched window above the stately front door opens out onto a small, wrought-iron enclosed balcony. I recalled for him that there had been a balcony, at this same level on the inside of the stately, chandeliered room.

He seemed impressed and invited me inside the front door. He told me he'd bought the building from the Walgreen family. The interior has been completely remodeled and is now an upscale apartment building. The foyer is comparatively tiny, as the first level is divided into four apartments, and a staircase ascending from the center, rear of the first level, leads to the apartments upstairs.

When I was ready to leave, the woman from Christian Care Services in the old Harrison House building asked for my address, indicating that she hoped I'd consider participating in the upcoming Founder's Day celebration. I gave her my address, and thanked her graciously.

Later I recalled the following poem, which I wrote about ten years ago in response to an annual tradition of the Episcopal Church where I've been a member most all my adult life. The poem recalls some difficult feelings I'd had in the Home, and embodies the essence of my conflicted emotions after again visiting the Home in spring 2000.

Here's a Christmas Child for You

I

At church we have this Christmas tradition
of providing gifts for the Children's Home.
Paper ornaments, on each a name is written,
dangle lifelessly form the branches
of the Parish Hall Christmas tree.
We are given scrupulous instructions:
"A sweater, slippers or anything
with the Panthers logo. Toiletries,
as long as they don't contain alcohol,
are okay." A very benign and generic gift.
We each pluck a child hanging from the tree
and next Sunday return its gift to place
underneath. Then all the gifts are delivered and
yearly the Priest praises our 100% participation.
Our cheeks smile;
our sanctimonious signing
swells the air.

II

This has been going on for many seasons:
I remember the church groups bringing gifts
and eats; parading through my Home.
Some would put on programs of singing and skits;
some groups would preach and try to convert us.
And now I must tell you a difficult thing:
we didn't like any of it.
We felt like freaks in a sideshow
as the tourists tramped through
clucking and muttering under their breath:
"Oh ain't it awful, Oh what a shame such
nice healthy intelligent good-looking
kids have to live in a Home."
Some of us demonstrated our rage by misbehaving.
That rascal Bud would scratch his armpits,

228

hop around on his haunches and growl "Ooo
Ooo, Ooo," in his deepest pubescent voice.
The tourists were horrified but we laughed
ourselves silly. How else to deny that
we were sad and lonely; hurt and afraid?

III
Some of the kids, their spirits long since broken
by the slings and arrows of outrageous fortune
or under the fist of some adult, were
quiet and withdrawn to the church groups
and to everything else. We knew the church folk
came to salve their conscience,
to cleanse their wealth.
Are you really surprised we knew this?
Soon the church groups no longer
came to gape at us; they had their gifts
delivered to the Home instead.

IV
Now I will tell you church people
what I would have wanted for Christmas.
Would you bring me to your house
for a home-cooked meal?
Nothing fancy; some hot, creamy, saucy food
like mashed potatoes and gravy will do.
Would you have me eat with your family—
just a normal meal with a typical family?
I promise I'd behave—
I'd be too intimidated by your abundance,
too awed by your lightness of life.
Would you share your richness of family with me,
discussing the day's events, the news?
And during the natural course of conversation,
would you inquire as to my interests, favorite
classes, college plans, what I might do with my life?
Because then you'd be suggesting my potential,

that I should apply, that I might even get accepted,
that I might have a future. I'd hear my heart pound
NoNo, NoNo, NoNo. I'd be taken aback by you
so easily suggesting these things to me
because I am so lonely and so afraid
and I don't have the confidence to dream.
Yes! Yes, Martin Luther King,
but it takes at least some
small measure of confidence to dream.
It takes some confidence to dream.

V
It takes some hope to dream.

VI
Where will I get this; how can I get this?
Would you have me gather with your family
'round the piano after supper,
join in the carol singing?
Invite me to play—I'd give anything
to have access to a piano.
I want to learn, I want to play.
Would you show me your favorite books,
the artful pictures; read me a poem?
And at the close of the evening
would you ask me for a photo of myself?
So that you could hold me in your heart
not just at Christmastime,
but all the year around.

***

Baseball is about coming home.

After I left Woodstock, and on my way back home to North Carolina, I wanted to stop in Chicago to visit my old neighborhood on North Pine Grove Avenue and to do some other sightseeing. I also wanted to go to Wrigley Field and see the Cubs play. After all, baseball is about coming home.

I drove the Mercedes to the Chicago Hilton on Michigan Avenue, recalling that it used to be called the Conrad Hilton. I visited nearby Roosevelt University and Buckingham Fountain across Michigan Avenue, the world's largest illuminated fountain. I visited the Art Institute and McCormick Place, the world's largest convention center. I ate Chicago-style, deep-dish pizza. I worked out at the Hilton's Health Club several times, and from my lakeside window on the twenty-fourth floor of the Hilton, I enjoyed the unexpected delight of seeing a spectacular Memorial Day fireworks show over the lake.

What a jewel in Chicago's crown is its thirty-one miles of sparkling Lake Michigan. After the famous Chicago fire of 1871, the city planners had the foresight to ban real estate development east of Lake Shore Drive, along the lake. Consequently, there are acres of parks and plenty of public access to the preserved natural beauty of the lake.

I was exhilarated and relaxed in Chicago, and even though I was in my old haunts around Roosevelt University, I experienced none of my agoraphobic anxieties of the 1970's.

I caught the Red Line to Wrigley Field and saw the Cubs play the Atlanta Braves. I bought a cap and tee-shirt and ate a Chicago-style hot dog with mustard, relish, tomato, onions—everything but no slaw, no ketchup and no chili.

From the ballpark, I walked east on Waveland Avenue. I passed by LeMoyne School at Fremont Street, where I attended kindergarten, and continued east, crossing Halstead Street. I came to North Pine Grove Avenue and then to the building we lived in, when we first came to Chicago, until it burned. I passed by many ivy-covered brick buildings—the neighborhood was even nicer than I remembered it to be.

I walked north to the Anshe Emet Synagogue and elementary school at a delightfully clamorous time; all the little children had just been let out of school for the day. Their parents were lined up along the curb in the narrow street in a Mercedes, Jaguar, Lexus or some such other expensive car. An attendant stood by the curb and as each car rolled up, a child's name was told to him from the parent-driver. Then he'd call out the name into a bull-horn, aiming it toward the chaotic crowd of kids in front of the school, and soon a book-bag-laden child shuffled forth to be directed to his parent's car.

19. A Visit to the Otherworld (2000)

What the Shaman Knows

Masculine
I have looked up the skirts of infinity
and death isn't such a bad ass.
Oh, she's hard, haggard and horrible
and within the lines on her face
are all the mysteries of life.
But underneath, her skin is velvet,
so surprisingly soft, smooth and supple.
And like all the other whores of life
she will cower when confronted.
She will spread her legs,
arch her back and draw me into her.
And I will pound her with my life until
she whimpers, shudders and feigns to come.
And while she lies in a self-indulgent
orgiastic heap, I will get up and walk away.

Feminine
While on sleep sheets
death slithered into me,
took me and had his way with me.
But I am strong like
the willow is strong.
I leaned into death,
surrendered to the darkness,
gave myself over to him
and went wafting up, up and away.
Death is a dumb fucker;
for even while he lies in
a disgusting, refractory heap,

I am nurturing the immortal
seed of life within myself.
For my time is short
but the children,
they are forever.

***

. . . for I myself do not have the answer when I per-
plex others, but I am more perplexed than anyone
when I cause perplexity in others.

Plato, *Meno*

On my way back to North Carolina from Chicago,
I stopped in Cambridge, Ohio to visit the gravesite of
my grandparents, Esther and Forest Webster Hall. As
I drove through Cambridge, my hungry eyes took in
everything, looking for anything that might stir up
memories from more than forty years ago—looking
for any sign of someone to whom I might be related.

I thought of well-known family names of clans in
the counties where I have lived and now live. I've
envied such people who have lived their entire lives
in the same town as did their parents, and their parents before them, and so on back for many generations. How wonderful it must be to call such a town
home because all your relatives on both sides, and
their families by marriage, all live there or are buried
there. I can hardly imagine such a sense of connection.

As I drove through Cambridge where my father
and I were born and where he grew up, and through
adjacent Muskingum County, where my mother's
family has lived continuously since 1824, I consi-

dered just how deeply rooted I am to the area.

I thought, *Well I should feel like I own this place, what with all my relatives who lived, and are buried here. This is supposed to feel like my home.*

So far in my genealogy research, I've been able to document the Hall's in Guernsey County, first in Quaker City then Cambridge, back to 1824.

Guernsey County was so named after the tiny island in the English Channel near the French coast, not after the bovine species.

The Hall's were Quakers, and came to Guernsey County, Ohio, coincidentally from North Carolina. And I can trace my father's mother's family also in Cambridge back to 1856.

But in the year 2000, when I drove there to visit, I knew nobody there to welcome me home.

***

Let us now praise famous men, and
our fathers that begat us.

Ecclesiasticus 44:1
The Apocrypha

Ah here is the Northwood Cemetery in Cambridge much larger than I would have imagined probably more people are here than alive in the town yes a stately brick archway entrance the wrought-iron fencing with its pointed arrowhead tips yes all very symbolic of entering another world and a tidy narrow road leads me inside the cemetery cloaked in green by many mature trees of various species big broad trees with muscular knotty trunks and the pink rhododendron bushes are in bloom now how am

I ever going to find you in this maze with no map I know only what section you are in the nice lady at the library got that information for me but this place has many sections and narrow circuitous roads meandering like infinity yes well of course how appropriate slowly wandering roads that give a sense of no time and space to me this cemetery is striking and lovely and makes me want to linger O yes every bit Elysium fields many American flags their crisp red white and blue colors so brilliant in the daylight trace the narrow road and energize the gravesites I think the pink rhododendrons are so soothing so comforting otherwise those broad muscular knotty tree trunks with big scary knotholes where they used to say the ghosts hid would make the place seem foreboding a sunshiny day sure does help too yes there are joggers and walkers taking their exercise making it all seem so natural life enjoying death and death enjoying life yes well here you are grandfather in such a pretty setting nearby is a rhododendron bush yes a very lovely setting which pleases me and your monument is stately and dignified and larger than most others and here it says The Reverend Forest Webster Hall and Esther Mariah Robey Hall does anyone reading these dates sense the grief of your short marriage and here all around you grandfather are your brothers and their wives and your sisters and their husbands I am pleased to find so many of you here yes I have come to visit you and Esther do you know who I am yes I am your eldest grandchild I am the first born of the only fruit of Esther's womb I remember once when I was a kid you stood up in a church service and introduced your son Paul and his family when we had come back to Ohio on the B & O railway train from Chicago to visit and when you introduced me you gave an explanation for my name being so similar to my father's you always

so quick with a joke yes you quipped that I was supposed to have been born a boy yes I remember that
got some titters from the congregation but I was
embarrassed and appalled as much as a shy beaten
kid could be well you know it takes some self-confidence even to be appalled yes I am a man now granddad though I was born a girl are you surprised that I
remember you telling that story in church well you
should have known to be careful of what you say in
front of a precocious child are you surprised that I
am a man now granddad well I want to tell you that
I have greatly admired you over the years and your
example has caused me to set my sights high yes in
some ways my life has been to restore your name
restore the integrity of our family name that your son
my father tried to trash did you know that in her
diaries Esther wrote while she and you were courting
that she referred to your father as an alcoholic yes I
see now that just as mine has been one of the pur-
poses of your life was to restore your father's name
and because of that we both were highly motivated
men I have thought about all of these things and it
must have been devastating for you to lose your
beloved Esther yes and I have those three diaries
that she kept before you two were married these are
the most precious books I have Phillip furtively got
them from our father your son and gave them to me
you see my father your son would not want me to
have these diaries or anything else of his or yours or
Esther's yes well I also have some of your handwritten notebooks and textbooks from Moody also surreptitiously gotten from him for me by Phil well so I
know how much she loved you and I know something
about the charming innocent spirit of the woman you
loved and all these many years later I am heavy with
the grief of her death I remember as a kid my father
your son ranting and lashing out at you with no

237

apparent provocation what could he have been so angry about why was he so angry at you or was he just angry at the world and God and projecting it all on you it seems that you should have been the angry one losing your dear wife Esther for a good-for-nothing angry epileptic son more persons than my mother have said that he was possessed by the devil yes I can see that too but it is hardly possible that a devil came from you and Esther the two most beautiful persons I have ever known gosh yes your faith must have been shaken to your core when you lost her and suffered other life disappointments such as your marriage and divorce to Virginia how scandalous for a Methodist minister in 1935 to be a cuckold and Paul's miserable life that he sabotaged every possibility that he threw away his musical talents and his other gifts including his children and his wife Joy that that made a mess of his life but despite many disappointments in your life you held up with grace yes and there have been some rude and insensitive people who have demanded to know why if my grandfather was so loving and so well off and so well connected and so resourceful why did he do nothing to save me why did he leave me to languish in the Children's Home well that question has always haunted me and Grandfather I have spent all my life not knowing the answer yes and now I want to know was there nothing you could do I remember you telling me that you would make sure I got a college education and I have never forgotten that yes well I know that you died just two years after we were put in the Home I am so lucky now to have a photocopy of your letter written to the Home saying you would like to take Esther and me into your home to live I cannot tell you how much that means to me I only wish I would have known about that letter as a youth what a difference it would have made in my life yes and I also have a letter written by your sister my Aunt Grace at about the same time also to the executive director of the Home in which she says how concerned she and all the family are and that they did not know that Paul had made us wards of the state she said she thought we were just boarding while our mother was ill in her letter she confirms that you asked to take us into your home to live it sure is healing for me to know all this now and not too late to thank you and yes I can easily imagine how it affected you to find out that your son had thrown away his children your grandchildren when you died I had just turned thirteen years old and I asked my mother the cause of your death and she said you died of a broken heart you such a proud and capable man how helpless you must have felt to find out about your grandchildren languishing in an orphans home and you possibly figured our lives were wasted I want you to know that I have had a rough life lacking parents I am talking about loving parents not sperm and egg donors yes but I have come here today to tell you that I have survived yes and just as you did I have restored our name Hall to honor not only have I have survived but I am a solid contributing citizen and not a burden on society as my biological father and mother are and yes well here I am telling all this to the spirits of the dead but at least now I have an answer to those who ask why if your grandfather was so great and so noble and so comfortably situated and so well connected and all that as you say why did he not rise up and save you yes well over the years I had to believe that you could not do anything to help me because of interstate laws or because of your age or some other reason dark to me yes well today I am sitting at your gravesite and I am willing to ask the tough questions yes and I am able to consider that if you knew me today you might

239

reject me here and now as your grandchild indeed you may have already done so at my birth because as you said I was supposed to have been born a boy I hold no man above my head and no man is perfect including me and you and every man has his vulnerabilities neither you nor I have been above my cynical scrutiny but I grant that you have come out well in my view that letter you wrote to the Home certainly does solidify my high opinion of you in the letter you wrote a year before your death you cheerfully detailed all your activities after retirement including twice weekly visits to the state hospital and once weekly visits to the Guernsey County Home then Thursday evening to the Contented Rest Home and regular visits to Bell's Rest Home and you visited two county hospitals and led an interdenominational men's prayer meeting on the second and forth Monday evenings and taught a Bible class on Sunday mornings at Ninth Street United Methodist Church and my goodness I am impressed most people retire to the golf course almost no one except Mother Theresa continues this level of regular ministry to the needy all through their retirement especially after they have done it all their life that would be considered much too physically exhausting and emotionally draining and most clergy and physicians are glad to be rid of those chores I find the story of your life truly inspiring for you to have endured several painful losses and disappointments in your life and yet you continued in faithful Christian ministry up to your death no matter what one believes or does not believe in the way of religion one has to concede that you did not live a self-serving life yes I only wish I had known of your letter as a child what an encouragement it would have been for me to know that you had tried to intervene to care for us in your home yes I know a cynic might say that you were involved in all

240

that ministry to the needy to make up for the fact that you did not want to or could not take care of your own grandchildren who were wasting away in an orphans home but I do not think that was so because you were involved in ministry to the needy all your life and long before I was ever born ah but now here you are dead and just as Telemachus said to Athene in the *Odyssey* no one really knows his father does this mean that no one knows the inner nature of his father or does this mean that no one can be sure of who his father is yes well whatever the meaning is I have considered that I do not know my father and I have wondered who my father really is and I have hoped he was someone else I still want to know why he hated you is there some secret reason why he hated you so much and why he hated me so much and not sister Esther yes I was the first born but is there some reason why he hated me so much other than the obvious that I was born female yes well know that I am willing to ask the tough questions is there something unique to you and me that he hated so I have thought of every possible answer to that question and the question does not bother me at all yes well I give thanks to God for you and your beloved Esther I am most fortunate and proud that you are my grandparents each of your lives has been an inspiration to me I honor you both and I am here today to pray you my highest tribute and yes well I hope you do not mind if I tell you that when I think of my parents it is you and your Esther who come to my mind O yes and the much-too-short love story of Forest and Esther is a most beautiful solo flower always trilling from the otherwise silent lonely fields of my life

In nomine Patris et Filii et Spiritus Sancti. Amen.

Part Eight

Wounded Healer

20. Wounded Healer

... even so, it is well with my soul.

from the hymn,
"It Is Well With My Soul"

Just before I began my appointment to medical staff at Duke University Medical Center on October 1, 1996, I reevaluated my career *vis-à-vis* my earlier perceived spiritual calling, and within the larger purpose of my life. I still believed that my medical employment was the working out of my larger spiritual calling, and this rang true for me now more than ever. I wanted to recognize my understanding of this in a special way, even if only between me and God.

A minister and counselor friend of mine encouraged me to present my medical ministry to the same universal fellowship which had ordained him. I did and was later ordained on August 1, 1996, in a simple ceremony held at the mountain-top home of one of the regional minister directors. It was a lilting outside ceremony. She had several hummingbird feeders, and while she spoke the words of consecration, a dizzying rainbow of hummingbirds buzzed and darted delightfully like mini-helicopters. Never before had so many hummingbirds come to visit me at one time.

So I have stayed true to my spiritual calling, to my satisfaction. I am a healthcare provider and my spiritual calling is worked out, in the hospital, at the bedside. I am licensed, registered, and certified to practice medicine; and I am also an ordained minister. And although the fact of my ordination is, for the most part, between me and God only, my ministerial credentials are as valid as the Pope's. I think it is much harder to be a priest or minister when no one knows that you are.

My profession now is considerably more fulfilling than the hospital ministry I'd envisioned fifteen years earlier while volunteering at the local hospital, and before attending seminary and then later medical school. For me, the two are a perfect meld of professions.

***

Myth of Me

I have a moist, woodsy-smelling memory
of the lady in the lake
with hair of flowing phlox
and petticoats of shimmering waves
she ascended through the waters
arms up-stretched,
a sword in her right hand.
She smiled and offered it.
As I swam toward her
she vanished in the morning mist
but the sword remained, floating.
I remember running through the forest
looking for the old man
to show him my sword.
He said, "Now your feet must dance on your toes
and your breath must sing through your face."
I remember when I found my inner voice,
the ringing sound of it,
the way resonance feels fuzzy
in my face and chest.
It was modulated with
the song of Calliope,
she still breathes me.
Without mother without father without offspring
without beginning or end of day,
I am both male and female,
I am as Melchizedek,
I am a priest forever
and I still have the sword.

***

246

As part of my work at Duke University Medical Center, I perform a minor surgical procedure. Pain control is achieved with a local anesthesia only, such as lidocaine, and the patient is usually not systemically sedated. Frequently, I can use only a local because the patient is too sick to be sedated: their blood pressure may be dangerously low, they may have fluid in their lungs or may otherwise be in respiratory compromise or distress, or their blood chemistries may be so deranged that vital organs are threatened.

The procedure has me at the bedside for at least thirty minutes and more time than that if difficulties arise. Many patients are conscious during this procedure and if so, within a short period of time, I must gain the patient's confidence and develop some rapport, because the patient must cooperate with me at least to the extent that he will lie still, flat on his back for the duration of the procedure. This is because I am placing a large bore catheter into the femoral vein, a large central vein in the groin, for an emergent or urgent blood-cleaning procedure, such as hemodialysis or plasmapheresis. Unless the patient is unconscious, he is frightened, anxious and frequently agitated.

Sometimes I must convince the patient that he needs the catheter placed and the subsequent blood-cleaning procedure, or else he will die very soon, maybe even in several hours. If something goes wrong during the procedure, the patient may be able to read my frustration or concern in my voice, eyes, facial expressions, and perspiration.

Sometimes while at the bedside, I am awash with compassion for my patients; as I have grown to the extent that I am able to feel compassion for myself. I have grown enough to be able to empathize with others' suffering without being overcome by it, instead of feeling only my own pain.

Most of my patients are utterly vulnerable and seriously ill. Many of them are marginalized and in addition to their several medical co-morbidities, they have significant psychosocial needs. Many of my patients are like those whom Jesus described "the least of these."

I know how it is to feel terrified, helpless, and alone, lying in a hospital bed tethered by a needle in my vein to an IV pole.

When I underwent my surgeries, I hoped that my surgeons, nurses, and techs would not expose me, neither my body nor my confidential medical record, unnecessarily.

I remember hoping that they would not make fun of my ambiguous body, but I realized they probably would, behind my back and while I was under anesthesia.

I had already learned that ironically, sometimes the most vulnerable and desparate people evoke the strongest hate and disgust from their caretakers. And so as a patient, I was always careful to present myself as a survivor, not a victim, and to be optimistic and positive in my manner. This was not always easy as I usually was discouraged and afraid, to say the least. But I knew that I certainly did not need to provoke such hate and disgust from my healthcare providers. And I did not want them to project their own sexual or gender insecurities onto me.

I prayed that my surgeons and other healthcare providers would not take any shortcuts, thereby increasing my risk of infection or other adverse outcomes. I hoped they wouldn't regard me as a "freak," using any other pejorative and depersonalizing labels, but would instead see me as a regular guy who was just trying hard to get along in life.

And even still, I have an ongoing, not entirely irrational worry that I may be unable to find any healthcare provider who will accept me as a patient, much less that they might be reasonably courteous, competent and experienced with, or maybe even just sensitive to my issues.

And as a healthcare provider myself, it seems to me an outrage that I've felt the need to crawl around to physicians, begging them to take me on, and always worrying that they won't. Many of my patients must also feel outraged and powerless in their own situations.

***

The other day I was waiting for a shuttle bus in front of Duke North Hospital. It was about 6:00 p.m., and many employees and visitors were leaving to go home. I saw a bevy of grey-white pigeons perched atop the nine-story, steel and concrete hospital.

And then, as if by some mysterious cue, they all lifted off together in a flurry of flapping wings. And like homing doves, they circled round and round the building several times, staying close together until they disappeared from my view.

I looked around me at all the people coming and going, and milling about. No one else seemed to have noticed this arcane group of air travelers. Musing idly while standing at the bus stop, I imagined that those doves were the souls of patients who had died in the hospital, and now they were departing for home. I always look for the pigeons on top of the roof when I pass by the front of the hospital, and I'm delighted when I frequently see them perched atop the roof—they seem to gather there more often in the early evening.

***

Many times my catheter placement procedures are done for patients in the intensive care units. These patients are frequently on breathing machines and other life support machines, and they are unconscious.

I remember coming back to consciousness after my first surgery, and in that ether-land state of mind. I could not move a muscle but my mind was surprisingly lucid and my senses were highly acute. I could hear and understand the voices of the nurses and techs. I could read the clock on the wall. The room smelled antiseptic and I felt cold. I was fully oriented to myself, time and place, but I could not have communicated anything. What a strange and somewhat frightening physical state of being. Fortunately it did not last long, as I soon vomited, which reflexively caused me to (try to) sit up, thereby awakening all my other sleeping muscles.

When doing my catheter procedures at the bedside of my intensive care unit patients, I frequently remember my own experiences in ether-land. I wonder what, if any, state of mind my patients are experiencing. I imagine that it is pleasant, much more so than we usually think. Those musings while at the bedsides of ICU patients, and seeing those spirit-doves flying from the hospital roof towards home, are the inspiration for the following poem:

Intensive Care Unit

My room's a garden.
See the hummingbird's
a shuttlecock over

the japonica tops.
Japanese Maple dances
in a crimson skirt

of delicate fringe, but
the jasmine are shy.
A solo flute plays

a bright fuchia tune.
Listen, Calliope breathes me.
And I am

a wild flying dove
just now released.
I leap into the blue

on vivace wings.
For I am
flying Home.

21. Searching for Hestia's House

I am a part of all that I have met;
Yet all experience is an arch wherethro'
Gleams that untravelled world whose margin fades
For ever and for ever when I move.

Alfred Lord Tennyson, *Ulysses*

It seems my life has been a constant struggle to find home—not only an inner home and to feel at home in my body, but now an external home as well. Sometimes we feel compelled to make sense of the seemingly random events of our life. We must find a myth or contrive a myth which gives insight into and purpose for our life. For me that myth is the struggle to achieve a sense of inner and outer home.

At age fifty, I've never had my own home. My parents never owned a home either. And so not only do I wish to participate in the American dream of owning my own home, I also have a compelling need to have my own home as the outer manifestation of my fully integrated self, my inner home.

Even though I've had no debt for years, have a down payment, and by objective standards have been reasonably secure in a stable career for more than ten years, I realize that for me, there have been other, more subtle obstacles to my buying a home than having a decent job, a down payment, good credit, and no dept.

In my early twenties, I developed an interest in building and real estate; I was thinking about buying my own home even back then, and I read every book on the subject I could get my hands on. It occurred

253

to me that I ought to have something to show for all that I'd learned.

In those days, one was not legally required to take a certain number of classroom hours of training in order to qualify to register for the real estate licensing exam. One could challenge the exam; all that was required was a realtor to sponsor you. So I went to a local realtor for this purpose; at the same time I was offered a part-time job in the office.

After several weeks of study, I took the train into Chicago and sat for the exam. When it was discovered that I'd passed the Real Estate Salesman License exam "on the first try" with no formal instruction, I was both regarded with awe and overtly snubbed by many in the office. The very next weekend, I saw my part-time job advertised for hire in the local newspaper.

I immediately went to the supervisor and asked why my job was being advertised without me knowing anything about it. This office manager was a woman at least twenty years older than I. She was tall and slender and though I'm sure she thought it attractive, she had a leathery face from too much sun-tanning. In clanging bangle bracelets, she fancied herself a wealthy socialite and flirted openly with the owner of the company.

When I approached her in her office she acted aloof, disinterested, and haughty. She regarded me as if I was the cleaning person; certainly I was someone she didn't believe worthy of her deigning to receive in her office. She would give me no explanation or reason but of course I knew. After I got my next paycheck, I didn't return.

***

Once I was fired from a summer job at a Mental Health Center when it was discovered that I had grown up in the Children's Home. I needed the money from the job and I was counting on the experience for my psychology degree requirements. Upon arriving at work one day, the supervisor called me into her office. She pleasantly and kindly told me that my work was excellent and beyond reproach but that she was "just following orders." She said "We didn't know you were from the Home; we just can't have that." No notice, no nothing. I was immediately dismissed and not allowed to return to my work area to say good bye to my co-workers. I was mortified and hopeless.

I lost a lot respect for the field of psychology after that. I was entering my senior year of college and I thought, *What good will it have done me to get a college education for myself if no one will hire me because of having the bad luck of irresponsible parents and because of them, a childhood in a Children's Home?*

From that point on, I carefully hid the fact that I'd grown up in the Children's Home. But nowadays, I proudly include it in my *curriculum vitae*. I have learned more from living my life, than I have from all the schools and training programs I've ever attended, combined and squared.

I know that "shit happens." However, I believe that this kind foul play is not as likely to happen to young people who are less vulnerable than I was, young people who have visible and supportive parents. Unfortunately, there will always be those who take advantage of, or even prey upon a vulnerable person of any age, especially when they look around and see that the person is alone, has no family or advocate.

Then when I was in PA medical school and for years after graduation, I anxiously considered that

255

after investing tens of thousands of dollars in my medical training, "someone would find out" about my gender reassignment and fire me or otherwise ruin my career. Living under the anxiety of being fired from a job because someone was threatened by my gifts of transsexualism or intelligence, keen insight into people, or survivor instinct; or was threatened because I had the audacity to succeed and didn't turn out to be a failure, like the psychology books said I would, is stressful beyond words.

I feared that I could work my ass off, overachieve, do everything right, be a shining example, and please everyone. But in an instant I could lose my job because someone didn't like something about me, and used my transsexualism to blackmail me or to fire me. I have always been alone with these types of worries. I've never had an advocate. I've never had a safety net.

It has been stressful and has taken all the character I could muster to keep hope alive and to persevere, without becoming totally overcome by pessimism and cynicism. And I realize now that all this had greatly affected my self-confidence in buying my own home, or more specifically, in taking out a mortgage.

***

When I met my wife, she'd been a widow for about seven years. She had just built a new home for herself with money from her deceased husband's estate. Her two children were grown and their college educations were paid in full.

At that time in my life, in early 1995, I'd completed my medical training and had been employed in my new career as a physician's assistant for three years. I had paid all my debts and maxed out my retirement 401 K and IRA. According to my life plans, my next goal was to finally buy a home.

Before we were married, I told my wife my dream of having my own home. I was sure that since she'd immigrated to this country at age twenty-one and later became a naturalized citizen, she'd certainly understand the notion of striving to improve one's life and to participate in the American dream of owning a home. She assured me that she did and it was reasonable to believe her. We decided that after no more than five years, we'd purchase a home together. I agreed, even though this seemed like a long time to further delay my lifelong dream.

Shortly after we were married, I received an appointment in the Department of Medicine/Division of Nephrology, at Duke University Medical Center seventy-seven miles away from our home. As five years passed quickly and thousands of commuting miles accumulated on my odometer, my lifelong desire to own a home became even more acute.

At the same time, it became apparent to me that my wife lost any interest she may have had in our plan of buying a home together.

By this time I no longer felt interested in, or obligated to, defend to her or anyone, my dream of having my own home. At the same time, however, I understood and accepted that she did not want to give up her home. I actually came around to the notion that I wanted her to keep her home. It would be better for me to buy my home separately and with my money only, perhaps closer to my employment. Most of all, I just want my own home.

As marital law is in our state, assets owned by a spouse prior to marriage, including interest and equity subsequently earned on those assets during the marriage, are solely that spouse's, and are not marital property. And therefore such assets then would not subject to equal distribution in the event of a divorce.

However, any assets accumulated during the marriage (not inherited, and not interest or equity earned on assets held before the marriage) are considered marital property.

In other words, any property that I might acquire during our marriage, such as the home of my life-long dreams, would be ours, not mine in the event of a divorce and would be subject to equal distribution. But her home would always be hers, never ours, since she had owned it before we were married.

This is totally unfair to me, and my hopes of buying a home seemed delayed indefinitely and certainly for as long as I was married. Under these circumstances, if I bought a separate home while married, she would continue to have the security of knowing that the home she'd owned before we were married would always hers, but any home that I bought would be ours, not mine. This is totally unacceptable to me. I do not plan ever to be kicked out of my home again.

There seemed to be no solution but divorce. I thought about this over the years, did a lot of research, and finally came up with an idea. It was to draw up a nuptial agreement; the same as a pre-nuptial agreement, except that it was drawn up six years after we were married. I sought out legal counsel and was greatly relieved to find out that this was indeed possible. I got four opinions from separate attorneys and each was puzzled as to why I didn't "just go ahead and divorce," but they all agreed that this would indeed be a solution to my problem.

This solution however would be useless if I could not convince my wife to sign such an agreement, which said in part that any and all property that I (or she) might acquire would be our separate property. Neither of us would have any claim to any assets of the other's acquired before or during our marriage. After several months, she agreed to these terms and agreed to sign the nuptial agreement. Six months later I had the signed document in my hand.

I felt victorious. This accomplishment did provide me immense relief and general peace of mind. I knew that I was now finally free to buy my own home, a home that I would never be kicked out of and that could never be taken away from me through divorce. And so far, I still had my marriage too.

I realized that when I bought my home, she'd of course keep hers and this level of separation might be stressful on the marriage, especially if I bought a home closer to my job. This was sad to consider, but I have never had a victory in my life which didn't also have significant compromise attached to it.

The chance to obtain a first home for myself at age fifty now seemed to come with the liability that I might not be able to keep my marriage at the same time. Good heavens! The nerve of me to think I could have everything—a marriage and my own home too!

On the other hand, there was also the possiblity that our marriage would be stronger after successfully getting through the six years it took to resolve this issue.

***

Hestia's House

On February 1, 2003, the space shuttle *Columbia* was tragically lost and all seven crew members perished. I am so sad—they were coming home too, and were so close. Though they didn't make it back to earth, they are home nevertheless.

259

Now after all this, I am still searching for my external home, and I know I'm very close. I think about it all the time. I can see it, inside and out, very clearly in my mind's eye. I will name my home Hestia's House after the Greek goddess of the hearth, and if I write this, it will come. It will be dedicated to the spirit of those who have striven to make it safely home. I already have a small sign which says "Hestia's House," to place in front, to welcome me home. I am so homesick for Hestia's House.

In Hestia's House there will be a great room with a broad brick hearth. There will be lots of windows and hardwood floors; there will be plenty of comfortable chairs and sofas. I will have my piano again that I've missed all these years. Hestia's House will be large enough, and many friends and family will all come to visit.

There will be a great library with many, many books; I already have many. There will be paintings, photography and other art pieces; I've a small collection already saved for my Hestia's House.

There will be a large table where we'll dine on hearty food. And after a generous meal, we'll sit in the great room drinking coffee, tea, or port. And we'll discuss literature, poetry, art, music, history, current world events, or news about friends and family. Someone will play the piano and sing. We'll stroll outside on the grounds, through the flower garden, down to a bee-loud glade.

I will have several pets: a little white West Highland Terrier named Toto, a noble black Labrador named Zeus, a loyal Golden Retriever named Argos and a calico cat named Calypso.

And if you, dear reader, find Hestia's House along your way, I wish you'd stop by, rest for awhile with me at my hearth, and tell me a story of your travels.

260

Epilogue

. . . Give me your tired, your poor,
Your huddled masses yearning to breathe free,
The wretched refuse of your teeming shore.
Send these, the homeless, tempest-tost to me
I lift my lamp beside the golden door!

Emma Lazarus, *The New Colossus*

This poem was written in 1883 by Emma Lazarus, as an invitation to Jewish immigrants. Though I'm not an immigrant, her poem is to me an exhortation to extend compassion and hope to those searching for home. These words capture the essence of the American spirit; and they inspire and comfort me.

Though not immigrants, my parents brought me with them from their well-established, secure family homes in the rolling hills of southeastern Ohio, to Chicago to make a new home. They failed miserably in their endeavor. Furthermore, bearing no accountability ever in their lives, they grossly defaulted in their parental responsibilities.

Fortunately in America, the sins of the fathers do not have to be visited upon their many following generations. In America a person has a chance to make some choices for his own life and there is hope here, like nowhere else.

Given my circumstances, I believe I would not have had a chance if I'd been born in another country. I wouldn't have had a chance to lift myself up from the scrapheap of society onto which my parents tossed me, much less the chance to dream of owning my own home.

And so I am America's child. America is my home.

261

Hestia's House

by Blaine Paxton Hall

Order Form

Ship To:

Name_____

Address_____

City_____**State**_____**Zip**_____

Phone Number (___)_____

E-Mail_____

Number of Books:_____@ **$24.95 each =**
Subtotal:_ $_____

NC Residents, add 6.5% Sales Tax:_$_____

Shipping & Handling, add $4.95/one book,
and $2.95/each additional book:_$_____

Total Enclosed:_$_____

Make check or money order payable to:
Hazelhurst House
P.O. Box 5427
Pinehurst,
NC 28374

Charge my Visa_____ **or MasterCard**_____
Card#_____

Exp. Date_____

Signature_____

www.HestiasHouse.com

My grandfather, Forest Webster Hall

My father, Paul Webster Hall

My mother, Joy Louise Harrop Hall

My parents, Joy and Paul Webster Hall.
This is their honeymoon photo.

The author, born Paula Joann Hall on July 9, 1952.
I actually remember these ducks very well. I was
pouting because my grandparents, who were
watching me, were trying to take the ducks away
from me because they were afraid I'd hurt myself
with the spikes. I was enthralled by the ducks and
I just had to play with them—to feel their shape,
and move them around. I must have convinced
the folks to let me play with the ducks after all.
Notice my scuffed knees and boy shoes.

**Sister Esther on left, and the author when as
Paula**

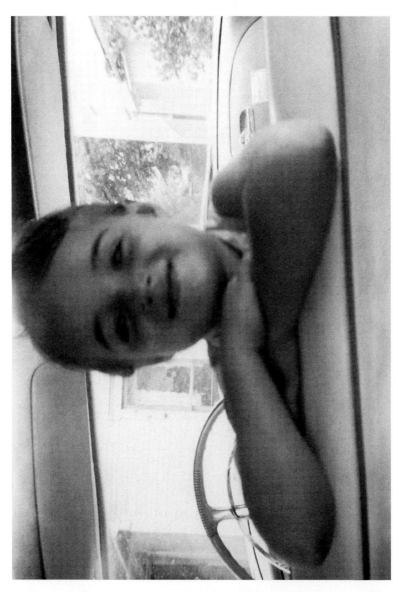

The author when as Paula, riding around with my Grandfather Hall in his Plymouth. He shot this photo of me from the back seat. I was so happy and proud to be with him.

Paula, age 7 ½ years old, facing camera.
Esther to my right. At D. R. Cameron School, Chicago.
Sister Esther is only eleven months younger than the
author.

**Paula on slide, showing the boys on the ladder
(right center) how to climb backwards up the slide.**
Clubhouse right center; notice the floodlights.

The original Children's Home

Original Children's Home

The original Children's Home
A different view

The Children's Home when I lived there in the sixties

Children's Home - shortly before being torn down - Feb. 25, 1983

The Children's Home just before demolition in 1983

Grace Hall in 1956, as it was named when owned by the Todd School.

This is the dedication ceremony of its new owner, the Woodstock Children's Home, and the renaming of the building to Harrison House, in honor of its benefactor.

The old Harrison House building in 2000.

Photo by the author in 2000

The demolition of the main building of the Children's Home, in 1983.

This was done to make way for Hearthstone Village, a senior citizen's complex.   *Sentinel* photo by Craig Schreiner.

THE WOODSTOCK CHILDREN'S CHORAL-AIRES

PERFORM IN WIDELY SEPARATED CITIES

The Woodstock Children's Choral-aires are gaining fame as a traveling choir. Under the direction of Mrs. Marvin Gearheart, they have recently performed in Peoria, Illinois, Milwaukee and Racine, Wisconsin churches.

The children and young people enjoy this medium of self expression and achievement. They have gained real poise and their program gives evidence of the many hours they have practiced.

Their repertoire includes secular and sacred numbers. They are available for service clubs, churches and other groups. Give them a call.

The Woodstock Children's Home Choir.
The author when as Paula, far right.
Photo from *The Woodstock Friend*

Rogers Hall, the only other extant building of the Todd School.

Photo by the author in 2000

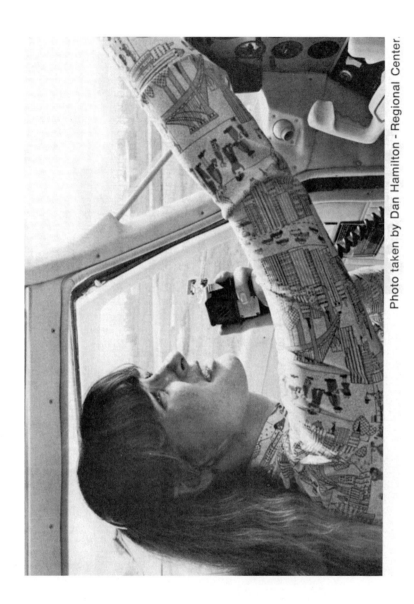

The author when as Paula, age 27.
I soloed in a Beech Sundowner.

Paula, age 28
This was during my Western Electric days,
leading a corporate management training work-
shop

The Opera House on the Square, Woodstock, IL.

Photo by the author's wife in 2000

The Square, Woodstock, IL.
Old Court House Building center background.
Photo by the author in 2000

The author on swing, on south veranda of the old Harrison House building.

Photo by the author's wife in 2000

My 1965 apple green, drop-top VW in the snow, in front of the Children's Home, Woodstock, IL.

Northwood Cemetery in Cambridge, Ohio, where my paternal grandparents are buried.

Photo by author in 2000

From left to right, my first cousins Howard Harrop and Carolyn Harrop, my brother Phillip Webster Hall and the author. We are standing in the Harrop homestead, where my mother and all nine of her siblings were born and grew up. Howard now lives in the old Harrop homestead.

Photo by the author's wife in 2001

The author, at Duke.
Photo by Marsha Mullis in 2000

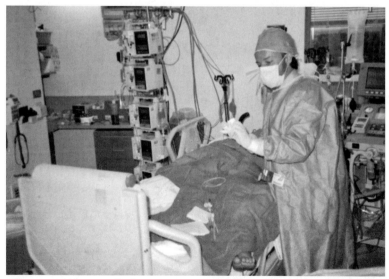

The author doing one of the 2,000 dialysis access vascular catheter procedures that he has done at Duke University Medical Center.

Math instructor Blaine P. Hall is a walking recruiter for his favorite course, Math Anxiety Reduction. Blaine cooked up his t-shirt just for fun and surprised his students by wearing the t-shirt with his sweat clothes to class one night. The back of the shirt carries the name of the course, the course number and the college name. "No one should be held back because they're nervous about math," Blaine said. "The strategies for overcoming that kind of fear are too simple."

Photo from *Inside CPCC,* 1985

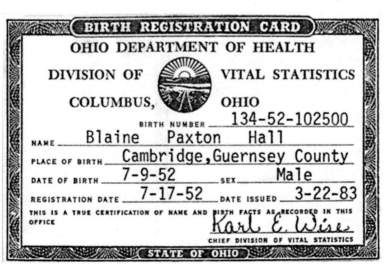

BIRTH REGISTRATION CARD

OHIO DEPARTMENT OF HEALTH

DIVISION OF   VITAL STATISTICS

COLUMBUS,   OHIO

BIRTH NUMBER __134-52-102500__

NAME __Blaine   Paxton   Hall__

PLACE OF BIRTH __Cambridge, Guernsey County__

DATE OF BIRTH __7-9-52__   SEX __Male__

REGISTRATION DATE __7-17-52__ DATE ISSUED __3-22-83__

THIS IS A TRUE CERTIFICATION OF NAME AND BIRTH FACTS AS RECORDED IN THIS OFFICE

Karl E. Wise

CHIEF DIVISION OF VITAL STATISTICS

STATE OF OHIO

Paula, Esther and Santa Claus